— THE —

RYDON GUIDE TO

ENGLISH
SPARKLING
WINE

— THE —

# RYDON GUIDE TO

# ENGLISH SPARKLING WINE

RYDON
PUBLISHING

A Rydon Publishing Book
35 The Quadrant
Hassocks
West Sussex
BN6 8BP

www.rydonpublishing.co.uk
www.rydonpublishing.com

First published by Rydon Publishing in 2021

A CIP catalogue record for this book is available from the British Library.

ISBN: 978-1-910821-33-6

## ACKNOWLEDGMENTS

Like any good vintage, this book has been some years in the making and in no small part owes its existence to the many wonderful vineyards producing fantastic sparkling wines across the UK. Thank you all for your contributions.

Special thanks to Simon Roberts of Ridgeview Estate and Rob Corbett of Castlewood Vineyard for their expertise, time, patience and enthralling insights into the wonderful world of English Sparkling Wine.

The team at IWSC for their great enthusiasm for the book, especially Dimple Athavia, Pip Mortimer and Kristen Dougall.

Julia Trustram Eve at Wine GB for her support of the book.

Thank you to George Chesterton at Finn Studios for the use of his beautiful images.

The wonderful team at Rydon Publishing. Dani Cowell, Ceri Jackson, Freya Grant and Olivia Huse for all their hard work, and finally and most importantly to Verity Graves-Morris and Prudence Rogers whose tireless effort and creative magic have created this beautiful book for you all to enjoy.

Cheers
**Robert Ertle – Publisher**

# CONTENTS

# Foreword

DELVING INTO the archives at the IWSC and dusting off the stapled sheets of tasting notes will reveal the history of wine trends from over 50 years. Uncovered are the wines and spirits that were popular in the seventies, as well as the trends emerging in consumers' drinking habits from the eighties and what countries and styles have been cemented by their continued success at the IWSC and other competitions.

In 1975, the winning wine from 'The British Isles' was mostly Sylvaner based, with Siegerrebe thrown in for good measure, a trend that was to continue for almost the next two decades. The first sign that the English wine industry was undergoing a renaissance came over 15 years later, in 1997, seemingly out of nowhere, when the first vintage of Nyetimber was received into the IWSC. Nyetimber Premiere Cuvee Blanc de Blancs 1992 entered and won a Gold Medal. Then in 1998 this former working farm went on to have their 1993 vintage crowned as the IWSC Bottle Fermented Sparkling Wine of the Year. Nyetimber went on to win this award a further three times, accompanied by Ridgeview Wine Estate in 2004 with their Merret Bloomsbury 2002. Both companies solely concentrating on sparkling wine from the hallowed trio of grapes used in Champagne, that is now seen as the jewel in the English wine crown.

It was this seal of approval within the industry that proved English Sparkling Wine was firmly on the map and here to stay from that point onwards, and the IWSC became a launching platform for several new English brands, many of whom are featured in this guide.

Over the next 12 years, from the early noughties to 2013, English wine entries grew by a staggering 220 per cent, with over 70 per cent of these entries being sparkling wine. The energy and growth saw no signs of slowing down, and the inevitable success of the English wine industry was confirmed when, in 2018, Ridgeview Wine Estate's Director of Winemaking, Simon Roberts, was named Winemaker of the Year – the top accolade given by the IWSC.

Since then, the IWSC English category has gone from strength to strength. In 2020, Langham Wine Estate won Sparkling Wine Producer of the Year, their success putting them ahead of fellow nominees from France and Italy. This was followed by one of the most successful English wine judging in IWSC history in 2021, with eight Gold Medals awarded to sparkling wines. Coates & Seely won the IWSC Bottle Fermented Sparkling Wine in 2019, while Gusborne won it in 2013.

The IWSC is proud to have been a part of the inception of the English wine industry, watching it grow to today's dizzying heights of success, where the best English Sparkling Wines rival top Champagnes in their gold-medal haul.

*Christelle Guibert*

CEO Fine Wine & Spirits

# INTRODUCTION

## BY SIMON ROBERTS
### Winemaker of the Year
### Director of Winemaking Ridgeview

Simon has been involved with his family's winery – Ridgeview – since 1995. Established on the foothills of the South Downs in Sussex, Ridgeview specialises in English Sparkling Wine, and the region is renowned for sparkling wine production.

Simon is a natural winemaker and prefers to let the grapes speak for themselves with quality overriding all decisions. In 2018 Ridgeview received the ultimate accolade by being named global 'Winemaker of the Year' in the prestigious International Wine & Spirit Competition.

## THE HISTORY OF ENGLISH SPARKLING WINE

Wine has been made in England since the Roman times – English vineyards were even mentioned in the Domesday book. After the Romans came the monastic communities who produced wine for their own consumption, followed by the grand houses of aristocracy. Winemaking in England is now witnessing a revolution due in no small part to the growing popularity of English Sparkling Wine.

However, the Traditional Classic Method of producing sparkling wine as it is known today really began in England in the 1600s, pre-dating sparkling winemaking in Champagne. A paper discovered in the Royal Society from 1662, written by Dr Christopher Merret – an English scientist – outlined the observation of creating a sparkling wine and the subject of secondary fermentation in the bottle, a good thirty years before Dom Pérignon. This process was fine-tuned by the monks in Hautvilliers, just outside Épernay which was the capital of the region of what later became Champagne. The 1600s also saw the development in England of strengthened wine bottles which enabled the pressures exerted

by Merret's process to be withstood.

The English Sparkling Wine renaissance that we are seeing now began in the late 1980s when American couple, Sandy and Stuart Moss, discovered the untapped potential of Southern England for producing world-class Traditional Method sparkling wine and founded what is now known as Nyetimber. Ridgeview followed suit in 1995 when my parents' (Sussex couple Mike and Christine Roberts) detailed research came to the same conclusion – that the cool climate and terroir of southern England would be perfect for sparkling wine production. With global winemaking trophies for the respective wineries, English Sparkling Wine soon emerged as a contender on the world stage. English Sparkling Wine was being served at some of the most prestigious events including the Queen's Diamond Jubilee, Royal Weddings and State Banquets. New sparkling wine vineyards began to appear across Britain, and existing still wine producers in England branched out into sparkling wine production.

Winemaking in Britain has exploded in recent years, with acres under vine having tripled since the year 2000. In 1995 there were just 984

hectares (2,432 acres) of vines planted, producing 1.7 million bottles of still and sparkling wine, whereas in 2020 there were 3,800 hectares (9,398 acres) planted (including plantings in 2021) and 8.8 million bottles produced.

Wine GB estimates that in 2021 English Sparkling Wine accounts for approximately 70 per cent of all wine produced in the UK, whereas in 1995 it would have been only around 10 per cent – a significant increase for a young industry.

Bottle production and yield will of course vary from year to year, with the weather having a significant impact. In the bumper harvest of 2018, 13.1 million bottles were produced.

This book guides you through a selection of English and Welsh vineyards in every corner of the country, showcasing the producers and celebrating their sparkling wines. Of the 65 vineyards featured in the book, several are often small-scale, so you can appreciate the hard work that has gone into producing their Sparkling Wine. The fruits of their labour are rewarded with a distinctive, individual style, which reflects their hard work, year in, year out. Many of the vineyards featured are remote, most of them are in areas of outstanding natural beauty, and some even have festivals. With a recent boom in English wine tourism, there's no better time to pay them a visit.

## GRAPE VARIETIES

The main varieties that go into making quality English Sparkling Wine are Chardonnay, Pinot Noir and Pinot Meunier. The creativity of blending these classic three varieties makes English Sparkling Wine so unique and exciting. Each grape brings different elements and structure to the wine which depend on the skills of the winemaker to bring these blends to life.

One of the major advantages of English Sparkling Wine is that we tend to get cooler, longer growing seasons, which gives the grapes fantastic natural acidity levels and the ability to age the wines to add complexity. Southern England and its terroir has proven – with global success – to be one of the most naturally suitable climates for sparkling wine production.

## CHARDONNAY
Citrus/tropical, Minerality, Freshness
Chardonnay is one of the world's most widely grown grapes, and brings particularly suitable characteristics for sparkling wine when grown in a cool climate. The citrus elements may bring grapefruit, crisp lemon or orange peel, with tropical notes possibly hinting of mango, melon or pineapple. Depending on the terroir of where the grapes are grown minerality, chalkiness and freshness may shine through.

One of the greatest aspects of Chardonnay is that it brings such freshness, which allows extra time for maturity while it is ageing in the cellar. Chardonnay is quite a hardy grape and of all the classic varieties tends to crop more reliably in our variable British climate with consistently good quality.

## PINOT NOIR
Red fruits, Finesse, Depth
The most capricious of the wine grape varieties, when grown well this red fruit can give wonderful finesse. The smaller berries often lead to a more concentrated flavour – Pinot Noir in a cool climate will show characteristics of black cherry, redcurrant and raspberry. Although there's not as much acidity as Chardonnay, it is still there which will give great backbone to the blends. When whole bunch pressing the red Pinot grapes, the winemakers are generally only looking for the white juice inside the red berry so a gentle pressing is required.

Pinot Noir is quite delicate and more prone to disease, therefore requires careful attention in the vineyard and doesn't generally yield so high.

## PINOT MEUNIER
Stone fruits, Richness, Backbone
The lesser-known, larger berried Pinot variety is one of the widest grown grapes in Champagne. Pinot Meunier is a workhorse of a grape with characteristics of both Chardonnay and Pinot Noir, therefore it is sometimes considered the

gel that brings the blend together. Expect cherry, strawberry and earthy notes with a slightly higher acidity than Pinot Noir and great aromatics.

Ripening a touch later than Pinot Noir, this red wine grape is often found in small quantities in sparkling wine blends due to its more concentrated fruit. Low in yield but big in body and richness, often contributing to the mid-palate and depth in the overall blend.

## THE VINEYARD CALENDAR

**January** Pruning – Pruning is such an important process in the vineyard, and will determine in a perfect year how much fruit the coming harvest will produce. The Vineyard Manager will use an equation measuring the fruit yield from the previous harvest to determine how much canopy to take off and how much to leave. Typically, 90 per cent of the previous year's growth is removed, leaving one or two canes to begin the new growth.

*As the new growth buds begin to emerge in Spring, they are very delicate and susceptible to frost damage so need protection*

**March** Tying down – This process creates the growth base for the coming season by tying down the cane left after pruning. Once the weather becomes warmer, sap will start to rise, making the canes more flexible. The canes can then be tied down along the bottom fruiting wire, setting up where this year's grapes will grow.

**April and May** Budburst – frost and frost prevention – This is the first major concern of the growing season. As the new growth buds begin to emerge in Spring, they are very delicate and susceptible to frost damage so need protection. There are many high- and low-tech solutions to help protect the vulnerable buds, from candles

and fans, to water sprinkler systems and electric cables. Although protection methods are costly, nothing is more costly than losing a crop to frost!

**June** Flowering – Vines are self-pollinating, therefore do not need bees or other insects to pollinate the flowers. However, most vineyards like to encourage biodiversity for both the environmental benefits as well as the overall health of the vines. What is required for flowering is warm dry weather; the more consistent the weather the healthier the fruit set will be to prepare the vines for the season. The more inconsistent weather or rain during this period may interrupt the fruit set and affect the size of the yield.

**July and August** Canopy management – The summer is spent tending to each plant; ensuring that each cane is positioned straight and upright, side-shoots cut-out, tops trimmed and the fruiting area managed so that air can flow freely. As a rule of thumb, each plant will be visited nine times, so

Over the summer, as a rule of thumb, each plant will be visited nine times, so with the average vineyard in the UK around 20 acres, that's a huge 22,000 plants

with the average vineyard in the UK around 9 hectares (20 acres), that's a huge 22,000 plants.

**September and October** Harvest – After the berries are formed, the fruit will grow for around 60 days until they their reach their peak. The Vineyard Manager and Winemaker will test the berries for perfect levels of acidity and sugar and then the harvest date will be decided. One of the main criteria for quality English Sparkling Wine is that the grapes must be hand-picked, pickers will be armed with a pair of secateurs and a small bucket, this is then emptied into a small picking tray to be transported to the winery for whole bunch pressing and processing.

## ENGLISH SPARKLING WINEMAKING

### Harvest/Blending

Once the grapes are received into the winery, they will be whole bunch loaded into the press, keeping each parcel of each variety from each site separate. The juice is extracted and left to settle in the tank for 48 hours, allowing sediment to fall to the bottom of the tanks. Yeast and sugar are added to the juice to create $CO_2$ and alcohol starting the first fermentation.

The first ferment lasts between 7–10 days and the resulting wine will have an alcohol content of around 10.5%. This makes a very dry base wine, perfect to produce Traditional Method sparkling wine.

After the base wines are fermented, they will be left to settle in the tanks or barrels prior to blending. The Winemakers will then take samples from all the different parcels across harvest to create the base wine blends. This is an incredibly difficult and skilful process where the Winemakers palate is crucial. Geology, vineyard microclimates and storage all play an important role in the

qualities of the parcels, adding to the complexity of the base wines to blend. The Sparkling Winemaker has to imagine what these wines will taste like in 2–10 years time, so a lot of skill and experience has to come into play.

## Cold Stabilization/Filtration

Once the blends are decided, the wine will be made 'cold stable' by removing tartrate crystals from the wine. This is done by adding cream of tartar to the wine and chilling the wine to -4°C. The crystals, when formed, will fall to the bottom of the tank and the wine is drawn into another tank. The wine is then filtered to make it stable by removing any sediment or yeast still present after fermentation. The wine is now ready for bottling.

## Bottling/Cellar

The secret of Classic Method sparkling wine is second fermentation in the bottle. On the day of bottling a tirage of sugar and yeast are added to the tank. The empty bottles are loaded onto the bottling line, filled with the wine, yeast and sugar and then sealed with a crown cap. The bottles are moved to the cellar where during the first six weeks they will undergo an individual second fermentation. The second fermentation needs a constant temperature and primarily to be conducted in darkness. This will produce more $CO_2$ and alcohol which dissolves into the wine, giving the wine its sparkle but leaving dead yeast (sediment) in the bottle. The alcohol content is raised by a further 1.5%, giving a general total ABV of 12%. The wines are left for anywhere between 18–48 months where the wine gains its traditional flavour profile, the longer the wine spends in the cellar the further development and richness it takes on – known as autolysis.

## Riddling/Disgorging

Once the wine is ready for release, the sediment must be extracted from the bottle. This process is known as riddling and disgorging. Bottles are laid horizontally into riddling crates that are inverted into mechanical gyro pallets. After five days of automatic twisting and turning in the machines the bottles are now upside down and the dead yeast will be captured in the neck of the bottle. The bottles are then carefully placed into a neck chiller that freezes the sediment. Now bottles can be upturned with the sediment frozen into the neck. The bottle goes through the disgorging line, where the cap of the bottles is taken off forcing the plug of ice (with the yeast) out of the bottle, leaving a clear wine. This is when the dosage, containing wine and a sugar solution, is added before finally being sealed with a cork ready for sale. The bottles are then left in stillages for a further three months before release to start to gain some cork ageing.

*The wine is then filtered to make it stable by removing any sediment or yeast still present after fermentation*

Once the wine is ready for release, the bottles are washed, labelled, packaged into boxes and palletised, ready to be enjoyed all around the globe.

## TASTING WHEEL

Should you be lucky enough to visit these vineyards, it is worth using a tasting wheel as a guide to enhance your wine tasting experience. A tasting wheel is a diagram of the many aromas and flavours that you might notice when sampling English Sparkling Wine.

Begin by holding the flute up to your nose and inhaling. Think about the aroma of the wine and look at the first ring of the wheel that best describes it.

For each word, look at the next ring of the wheel to further refine your description. Finally, follow the descriptive word to the next level of the wheel. Next, take a sip of the sparkling wine, and hold it in your mouth for a few moments before swallowing so that you can sense several different flavours. Use the wine wheel in the same way that you did for the aroma. This will help you to describe the wine, give you an idea of what to look for, and most importantly what you like about English Sparkling Wine.

## HOW TO USE THIS BOOK

Each vineyard showcased in the book have their own unique features. Every vineyard entry has information on the terroir, their history and the types of grapes they grow. The entries are also accompanied by a handy key, which summarises the important facilities:

 Accommodation

 Café / Restaurant

 Children Welcome

 Disabled Access

 Dogs Welcome

 Electric Car Charger

 Online Shop

 Organic / Biodynamic

 Outdoor Eating

 Tours Available

 Venue Hire

 Vineyard Trail

 Weddings

 Winery on Site

# SOUTH WEST

The South West vineyards grow a greater range of grape varieties using differing production techniques, so expect to find authentic, individual, terroir-driven wines in the most rural and beautiful destinations.

Trevibban Mill
Vineyard & Orchard

Camel Valley Vineyard

Polgoon Vineyard

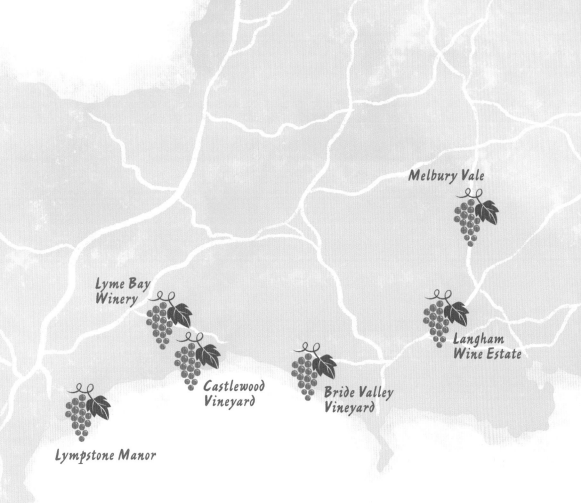

Melbury Vale

Lyme Bay
Winery

Langham
Wine Estate

Castlewood
Vineyard

Bride Valley
Vineyard

Lympstone Manor

Sandridge Barton Wines

# *Spotlight on*
# BRIDE VALLEY VINEYARD

## DORSET

STABLE COTTAGE, THE COURT HOUSE, LITTON CHENEY, DORSET, DT2 9AW

- **10.2 Ha of planted vines**
- **30,000 bottles annually**
- **Winemaker Ian Edwards**
- **Grape varieties Chardonnay, Pinot Noir, Pinot Meunier**

## TERROIR

Steven and Bella Spurrier made Litton Cheney their Dorset home in 1987 and from early on Steven was keenly aware of the potential for growing vines on his wife's 200-acre farm on the edge of the village, little more than a stone's throw from the World Heritage Jurassic Coast.

The clean chalky Kimmeridgian soil was almost identical to that found in the Champagne region of France; the village of the same name being just 24 miles away. The fine south facing slopes offered a favourable climate for the cultivation of Chardonnay, Pinot Noir and Pinot Meunier vines.

Having spent a lifetime in the trade the opportunity to produce his own wine grew too much for Steven to resist and in 2009 forty-four thousand vines were matched to the climate and subsoil and planted over 25 prime acres of the farm.

## ABOUT

Steven Spurrier, who sadly passed away in spring 2021, was one of the most influential and celebrated individuals in the wine industry. Joining the London wine trade in 1964 he later moved to Paris where he bought a wine shop in 1971, and opened L'Académie du Vin, France's first private wine school.

In the 1980s he wrote several wine books and created the Christie's Wine Course with Michael Broadbent. In 1988 Steven returned to the UK to focus on writing and consultancy and authored a number of books alongside his role as consultant editor for *Decanter* magazine.

However, he is most widely recognised as the mastermind behind the Paris wine tasting of 1976, universally known as the Judgement of Paris – an event which revolutionised the world of wine.

The English Wine industry, wine tourism and interest in the provenance of food and drink have all seen exponential growth in recent years, and so to accommodate the growing number of visitors, Bride Valley Vineyard has invested in a dedicated art and tasting room. Here Steven's cornucopia of pictures, artefacts, and array of awards collected during his 50+ year career, are on display for all to enjoy. The Cellar Door is also housed here, all within a charmingly converted stable block opening onto the tasting room gardens where Steven's collection of sculptures nestle comfortably in their surroundings.

## THE WINE

### Blanc de Blancs

Bride Valley Vineyard's signature wine. 100% Chardonnay – elegant with purity and precision. This is the wine synonymous with Steven Spurrier and Bride Valley Vineyard.

### Dorset Crémant NV

England's first Crémant. Creamy gentle mousse which 'dances' on the tongue. A wonderful aperitif. Described as "a wine that sparkles, rather than a sparkling wine". This wine, which holds its own Protected Designation of Origin (PDO), is proving immensely popular both in its own right and as an alternative to the classic sparkling wines.

### Rosé Bella

A combination of Pinot Noir and Chardonnay, its refined flavours make this a joy to drink. Produced since 2011, this wine was named after Steven's wife, Arabella. The 2018 vintage is an amazing reflection of the amazing fruit and harvest of that year.

### Brut Reserve

A classic blend of Pinot Noir, Pinot Meunier and Chardonnay grapes make this a great all-rounder suitable for any occasion.

## VISITING AND BUYING

Wine available via online shop or at Cellar Door. Visitors are welcome for pre-booked tours and tastings between April and September. Please check website for opening times.
**www.bridevalleyvineyard.com or email info@bridevalleyvineyard.com**

# Spotlight on
# CAMEL VALLEY VINEYARD

## CORNWALL

CAMEL VALLEY, NANSTALLON, BODMIN CORNWALL PL30 5LG

- **10 Ha** of planted vines
- **150,000** bottles annually
- Winemaker **Sam Lindo**
- Grape varieties **Pinot Noir, Chardonnay, Seyval, Rondo, Dornfelder, Bacchus**

## TERROIR

Camel Valley became the first UK wine producer to receive a Protected Designation of Origin (PDO) from the European Union. Soil is a medium loam over ancient slate and the aspect of the vineyards, all planted on steep South-facing slopes, running down to the River Camel. The vineyard is situated exactly in the centre of Cornwall, 16 kms (9.9 miles) equidistant from both the Atlantic and the Channel Coasts. The growing season is long and beneficially affected by the Gulf Stream. The Camel River Valley has historically a better climate than the rest of Cornwall.

## ABOUT

When ex-RAF pilot Bob Lindo and his wife Annie planted their first 8,000 vines by hand in 1989, they never dreamed of the phenomenal success that they would achieve within three decades. They had bought their farm in the heart of the Cornish countryside several years earlier, seeking a change from service life and the perfect place to bring up their young family, and initially farmed sheep and cattle. Each summer they watched the grass turn brown on the sun-drenched slopes of the Camel Valley, and wondered if vines might enjoy such an aspect.

Bob won the UK's first International Wine Challenge Gold Medal (presented in Bordeaux) in 2005. The Lindos are now second-generation producers and a wine-making family with 30 years of experience. Son, 'born in a barrel' Sam, became winemaker in 2006 and from 2006 to 2011 Sam won the 'UK Winemaker of the Year' trophy three times and was runner up on the other two

years. Together, they hold five International Wine Challenge trophies, including the International Trophy for the best Rosé sparkling wine (including Champagne) in the world. They have also won four Italian Bollecini Del Mundo Trophies. Bob was awarded the International Wine Challenge Lifetime Achievement Award trophy in 2018.

Also, in 2018 Bob was awarded a Royal Warrant and Camel Valley sparkling wines are now 'by Royal Appointment' and served at many prestigious Royal and Government occasions.

The vineyard has been featured in numerous films and TV shows including: *Rick Stein's Food Heroes, The Paul O'Grady Show, 'Let's Do Lunch', Caroline Quentin's Cornwall, James Martin, Saturday Kitchen, Alan Titchmarsh, Delia Smith, Raymond Blanc's Christmas, About Time, Nathan Outlaw*, and many others.

## THE WINE

### 2018 Camel Valley Cornwall Brut
A fresh and fruity traditional method sparkling wine, perfect for all celebrations.

Fresh yeasty aromas, English hedgerow scents with good acidity and a touch of honey on the palate.

Served in Rick Stein's world-famous Seafood Restaurant and Nathan Outlaw's iconic two Michelin Star Restaurants.

This Cornish sparkler made by Sam Lindo will be served in British Airways First Class.

### 2018 Camel Valley Pinot Noir Rosé Brut
Beautifully balanced light pink, traditional method sparkling wine with classic English Pinot character.

Lovely floral and delicate strawberry fruit nose and crisp acidity.

The 2010 vintage won a Decanter World Wine Award Gold medal, the UKVA Trophy for the best Sparkling Rosé in England and was awarded first place in the MWs tasting of 90 English Sparkling wines in 2012.

The 2008 and 2009 vintages were both outright winners of the Sparkling Rosé International trophy in Verona (Bollicini Del Mondo). Camel Valley 2009 Pinot Noir Rosé was crowned Sparkling Rosé World Champion ahead of Bollinger Champagne Rosé and also won the International Wine Challenge Trophy.

### 2016 Annie's Anniversary Brut
Zippily fresh, lemony and tropical, with richer, yeastier depths.

There are very few vineyards in the world that have only ever been pruned by just one person and Annie Lindo is one of those select few. To commemorate her 100,000th vine pruned, the millionth cut by hand with secateurs, and her 20th vintage, her son, 'UK winemaker of the year' Sam, made this anniversary cuvée and it was featured on Caroline Quentin's Cornwall.

Like her 2009 wine, the 2010 was also awarded a Gold Medal. Decanter gave it a mammoth 18/20 points and the 2010 won its Gold Medal and the Lord Montague Trophy in the Wine of the Year Competition.

### 2015 White Pinot Noir Brut
An elegant sparkler with a pearlescent hue, a fine filigree mousse, with youthful Red fruits on the nose and a fabulously long finish. Traditional method quality sparkling wine made with Pinot Noir - Blanc de Noir!

International Wine Challenge 2018 Silver medal winner.

Made exclusively from Pinot Noir grapes harvested from their Barn field plot, situated next to their winery.

### 2017 Cuvée Raymond Blanc de Noir, Rosé Sparkling
The 2014 Rosé sparkling was crowned 'World Champion', Bollecini Del Mondo (Italian World Sparkling Wine Competition, held in Bardolino 2016). Raymond Blanc de Noir Rosé was made to celebrate Raymond's visit to Camel Valley to film 'Raymond Blanc's Christmas'. Raymond picked grapes at Camel Valley and helped load the press himself.

### 2014 Camel Valley Sparkling Demi-Sec
Sweet apple blossom, sherbet and honeysuckle combine elegantly in this lively, sweeter style of fizz.

### 2014 Camel Valley Chardonnay Brut
A classic Blanc de Blancs. This Chardonnay sparkling wine delivers a fine mousse, gentle citrus flavour and a light toast finish.

## VISITING AND BUYING

**Opening Times: Wine Sales – 10am–5pm. Year-round Monday to Friday Including Bank Holidays. Always closed Sundays. Opening times may vary.**
**Sorry No Dogs, Except Guide Dogs.**
**See www.camelvalley.com for up to date hours and tours.**
**Telephone: 01208 77959**
**Email: info@camelvalley.com**

# Spotlight on
# CASTLEWOOD

## DEVON

CASTLEWOOD VINEYARD, CASTLEWOOD FARM, MUSBURY, AXMINSTER, DEVON EX13 8SS

- **3 Ha** of planted vines
- **8,000** bottles annually
- **Winemaker** Rob Corbett
- **Vintage information** Castlewood Vintage Brut 2017, Devon Minnow 2018
- **Grape varieties** Pinot Noir, Chardonnay and Pinot Meunier represent three quarters of the oldest vineyard with 'varietals' mainly of Germanic origin representing the rest. In 2016 a further 2 Ha of Bacchus were planted

## TERROIR

Castlewood Vineyard emerged from its south-facing Devon hillside between 2006 and 2009. The vineyard's aspect is directly due south on a rolling slope. This enables any cold air to gently flow to the valley floor, providing a frost-free environment in which the vines flourish. Their fertile clay-loam soil drains freely through the subsoil into a stream that runs along the southern boundary of the vineyard. Planted at a low vine density, Castlewood's three-metre row widths help prevent row-to-row shading. As the sun reaches its summer heights the vineyard achieves maximum sunlight hours. Close grass cover manicured throughout the year not only aids soil structure but also prevents soil erosion during the winter months.

## ABOUT

This pocket of only a few thousand vines maintains its quality by only using the ripest fruit which deliver the optimum flavours for their exclusive sparkling wine. The vineyard is owned and managed by Rob Corbett who meticulously tends to every vine throughout the growing season. They call in the labour of family and friends for the harvest, with everyone eagerly anticipating the coming vintage and their free wine as payment.

## THE WINE

All of the wines are made without filtration or the use of any fining chemicals. They undergo a minimum of 18 months secondary fermentation before release. Due to its small scale production Castlewood leave their wines to clarify naturally in stainless steel, oak barrel and more recently clay amphorae. Their old stone buildings provide a cool constant temperature enabling the perfect environment for maturation.

### CASTLEWOOD NV BRUT

The Non-Vintage blend will often comprise the 'varietals' Seyval Blanc, Madeline Angevine and Reichensteiner. Germanic in origin these varieties ripen before the noble Pinot Noir, Chardonnay and Pinot Meunier. After gentle basket style pressing the must is cold fermented in small scale vats. These varieties that make up the NV have often fermented to dryness before its remaining constituent varieties have even been harvested. Once picked and pressed the tailles (second pressings) from the Pinot Noir, Chardonnay and Pinot Meunier are cold fermented separately ready for assemblage with the varietals.

### CASTLEWOOD NV ROSÉ

The Rosé blend has only been introduced since the 2013 vintage, comprising Pinot Noir and Pinot

quality. A gentle bladder press of greater volume is used to ensure a slow but delicate extraction of the vintage cuvée. Second and third pressings (the taille) are separated for the Non Vintage blend. Overnight cold settling procures a crystal-clear must prior to cold fermentation. About a fortnight to one month later, the Chardonnay is picked. At the time of writing the current Vintage is 2017, comprising 65% Pinot Noir and 35% Pinot Meunier.

### BRUT NATURE 2018

A true expression of Castlewood terroir in its purest form. Depicted on the label is the Growing Degree Day (GDD) curve for Castlewood Vineyard. It displays the average daily air temperature above 10C cumulatively over the 2018 Vintage. Being zero dosage it expresses the very essence of both grape varieties of Chardonnay and Bacchus in a generous yet crisp mineral style. Bright aromas of elderflower and fresh cut grass, green citrus fruits and ripe lemons with a flinty minerality. An elegant and complete sparkling wine.

## CASTLEWOOD WINE FESTIVAL

Each year, the harvest from the boutique vineyard is enjoyed in the form of an annual Wine Festival in early June. They showcase all of their wines, from the latest vintage release and invite neighbouring vineyards to join in too. Combined with an array of local food and musical talent from farther afield it's a great weekend. Tickets go on sale in early March and usually get snapped up quite quickly!

## VISITING AND BUYING

Open by appointment. Events are also held from time to time in conjunction with nearby River Cottage. As well as the small vineyard, the main business here is dairy farming and two holiday cottages are also available to rent.
**For all enquiries, please contact Rob Corbett.**
**Email: info@castlewoodvineyard.co.uk**
**Telephone: 01297 552068 / 07812 554861**

Meunier and on occasional years the 'varietals'. Like the NV, 'the varietals' ripen earlier, providing riper red fruit characters, often preferred in Rosé blends. On assemblage, the NV wine is blended according to taste and colour to make the Rosé. Pinot Noir and Pinot Meunier provide the driving fruit character, ever present in the noble varieties. Like all Castlewood sparkling wines, the NV Rosé undergoes traditional method secondary fermentation for a minimum of eighteen months before release.

### CASTLEWOOD VINTAGE BRUT

Vintage blends are made only from exceptional years, solely from the noble varieties. Pinot Noir and Pinot Meunier usually ripen within a week of each other. A sensible mid point is chosen and grapes picked depending on weather conditions and fruit

# LANGHAM WINE ESTATE

## DORSET

THE TASTING ROOM, LANGHAM WINE ESTATE, CRAWTHORNE FARM, CRAWTHORNE, DORCHESTER, DORSET DT2 7NG

- 11 Ha **of planted vines**

- **50,000** bottles annually

- Winemaker **Tommy Grimshaw**

- Vintage information **currently selling 2017 Blanc de Blancs, 2018 Pinot Meunier, Rosé NV and two non-vintage cuvées Culver and Corallian**

- Grape varieties **Chardonnay, Pinot noir, Pinot meunier**

## TERROIR

Located east of Dorchester, on a south facing slope at approximately 85 metres (278.8 feet) above sea level and protected from prevailing weather by a band of mature woodland, their 11-hectare vineyard site was planted in 2009. The soils are composed of a shallow clay loam overlying a dense bedrock of cretaceous chalk strata. The sponge-like structure of chalk provides good drainage during episodes of heavy rain, but also a reservoir of water for the vine roots during dry periods. Two of these strata, Corallian and Culver, give their names to their Classic Cuvées. These chalk soils bring a fresh, saline character to the wines, and by reducing inputs both in the vineyard and winery they hope not to cloud these characters.

## ABOUT

At the heart of the Langham Estate sits the magnificent Bingham's Melcombe manor house, Grade I listed and little changed since the reign of Edward VI. Acquired by John Langham in 1980, Bingham's Melcombe became the centre point for the Langham Agricultural Enterprise, today comprising over 1,000 hectares. It was John Langham who originally established a very small-scale vineyard on his land. In 2009 John's son, Justin Langham, decided to build on his father's idea and develop the idea of a vineyard into a commercial venture. He eventually planted 30 acres of vines on their land at Crawthorne Farm, just a few miles from Bingham's Melcombe house.

## THE WINE

As winegrowers, they pride themselves in crafting terroir-driven sparkling wines using grapes only grown on their Dorset vineyard. They take a low-intervention approach to both grape growing and wine production, constantly striving to minimise their environmental impact and produce honest wines that reflect their terroir. Their wines are fermented in a mix of ex-Champagne, Burgundy and Bordeaux barrels (3–25 years old) and stainless-steel vats and left to rest on the spent yeast lees over the winter months before finishing the primary fermentation in spring. The wines are bottled in early summer without being filtered and with minimal sulphur dioxide.

The culmination of these methods is a range of exceptional quality wines which consistently impress sommeliers, wine critics and judges alike. Langham Wine Estate was overjoyed to have been awarded the trophy for Sparkling Wine Producer of the Year at the IWSC 2020, fighting off competition from renowned French Champagne houses such as Maison Mumm and taking the trophy from 2019's winner Veuve Clicquot.

## CULVER CLASSIC CUVÉE NV

A blend of 55% Pinot Noir, 20% Pinot Meunier, 25% Chardonnay, the vast vintage is from 2018 with 11% reserve wine. The focus of this Pinot Noir dominant member of the Langham Core Range offers up Pink Lady apple notes, floral elements, a broad palate and aromas of butter croissants and raspberry jam.

## CORALLIAN CLASSIC CUVÉE NV

A blend of 75% Chardonnay, 15% Pinot Noir, 10% Pinot Meunier, the base vintage is from 2018 with 17% reserve wine. The focus of this Chardonnay dominant cuvée is fresh apple notes, a crisp citrus acidity and a saline thread.

## ROSÉ NV

There are Rosé aromas aplenty with cherry bakewell, Pink Lady apple skin, raspberry yoghurt and wild strawberries. The palate reflects this fresh red berry profile, but it is also more serious and has great depth. Cherry yoghurt, young wild strawberry and raspberry coulis bring the fruit profile to the forefront, while a more savoury, saline note of habas fritas rounds off this delicious wine.

## BLANC DE BLANCS 2017

Using 100% Chardonnay from 2018, this wine was aged on lees for a minimum of 30 months. There has been no sulphur added to this wine. This wine offers up floral notes of apple blossom and honeysuckle, along with Gala apple. A seriousness here too, with wet beach pebbles and toasted granary bread.

## PINOT MEUNIER 2018

A rare example of a single varietal 100% Pinot Meunier from 2018. The nose is intense and pronounced. Caramelised peach, fresh cream and wet beach pebbles come initially. These aromas are backed up by a delicate wave of floral notes, such as apple and orange blossoms and honeysuckle. The palate is rich and complex with a profile of white peach, pear tarte tatin and salted almonds.

## VISITING AND BUYING

They have a Tasting Room, Café and Shop open all year round for tours, tastings and events. **Please check their website for up-to-date information www.langhamwine.co.uk**

# LYME BAY WINERY

## DEVON

LYME BAY WINERY, SHUTE, AXMINSTER, DEVON, EX13 7PW

- Area Varies

- 10,000 bottles annually across all sparkling production

- Winemakers James Lambert, Sarah Massey, Nathan Maddocks

- Grape varieties Bacchus, Chardonnay, Pinot Noir, Seyval Blanc

## TERROIR

Lyme Bay Winery works with experienced vineyard owners all over the country on long term contracts to source the best possible fruit from the best growers in the best vineyards, rather than owning their own. This allows them to make long term planting and sourcing plans with their growers and gives them the confidence to get the right quality and yields that they need to make the best possible wines.

It also allows them to adjust for the marginal climate in the UK. This means that they are less likely to be a victim of the sometimes challenging weather patterns in the UK including frost, rain and hail and allows them to source fruit from different parts of the country, from Devon to Herefordshire, through Essex and Kent to ensure that they can always deliver the highest quality every vintage.

## ABOUT

Lyme Bay Winery is the home of LBW Drinks. Their small, dedicated drinks company is full of people who are passionate about producing delicious and award-winning English Wine, Fruit Wine, Cider, Mead, Liqueurs and Spirits from their home in Devon's beautiful Axe Valley.

They combine knowledge and love of flavours and ingredients with their wine-making skills to craft award-winning traditional drinks, tailored to the 21st-century palate. Each of these amazing products is fermented, blended and aged, as appropriate, at their Winery under the supervision of their experienced team.

## THE WINE

Lyme Bay Winery is the only English Winery to achieve an A* accreditation for manufacturing quality from the British Retail Consortium (BRC) ensuring that all of their products are crafted to the highest standards.

They source grapes for their English Wines from select growers across the country so that they can confidently claim to make the best wines from the best grapes from the best growers – every time.

They are also a significant producer of mead in the UK, and have recently innovated in this sector by producing mead and cyser (a blend of mead and scrumpy cider) in cans for the first time.

### Brut Reserve Sparkling – NV
Their Brut Reserve English Wine is a fruit-driven sparkling wine that displays refreshing lemon and green apple notes, with a vibrant and creamy mousse finish.

### Sparkling Rosé – NV
A sparkling Rosé made from Pinot Noir grapes, boasting a bright, fruit-driven palate with a richness of honey and hints of brioche.

### Classic Cuvée – 2016 New Vintage Release
The Classic Cuvée is an elegant sparkling wine, showing a depth of citrus and stone fruits flavours, along with the more complex secondary aromas of cooked apples, breadcrumbs, honey and almond.

## VISITING AND BUYING
SHOP OPENING TIMES
Monday – Saturday: 09:30 to 16:30
Please check website before visiting.
Buy online at www.lymebaywinery.co.uk
Telephone: 01297 551355
Email: info@lbwdrinks.co.uk

# Spotlight on
# LYMPSTONE MANOR

## DEVON

LYMPSTONE MANOR, COURTLANDS LANE, LYMPSTONE, DEVON EX8 3NZ

LYMPSTONE
MANOR

Hotel | Restaurant | Vineyard

- **17,500 Ha** of planted vines
- **Vineyard Manager James Matyear**
- **Grape varieties Chardonnay, Pinot Noir and Pinot Meunier**

## TERROIR

The vineyard has been mapped out to determine the best row orientation to maximise available sunlight. The soil was enriched with organic compost and lime. Because it had been many years since the land was last cultivated, the ground had become compact, so subsoiling was necessary to reinvigorate the earth to bring oxygen back into the earth. This was followed by a final plough, turning the soil to allow it to break down over winter in anticipation of planting in the spring of 2018. 18,000 Chardonnay, Pinot Noir and Pinot Meunier vines were planted at the optimum moment in April 2018.

## ABOUT

The first small harvest was in October 2020. Afterwards, the laborious process of turning the subsequent still wine into quality sparkling wine by the classic method of secondary fermentation in the bottle, including ageing on the lees for 2 years to add complexity, will be equally painstaking and time consuming.

It is anticipated that the first release of Lympstone Manor Cuvée will not be before October 2023.

## THE WINE

Michael Caines MBE had a dream to produce high-quality English Sparkling Wine utilising the varietals of Champagne: Pinot Noir, Chardonnay and Meunier. Vineyards, like dreams, take time to be transformed into reality, time for roots to penetrate deep down and become established, time for grapes to ripen, for wines to be made, for secondary fermentation, and for the complexity to develop that only comes from lengthy maturation on the lees in the bottle.

In May 2018, the first stage of the dream was realised: 17,500 vines are now planted in the Red earth of Devon, basking in a special and protected micro-climate that has been identified as one of the very best in the country. The first significant harvest is unlikely to be before 2021, and it will take a further two years for the wines to develop and mature before release.

"The vine likes to see the water", asserts Michael confidently. "Most of the great vineyards of Europe are all located near rivers, the Médoc châteaux of Bordeaux on the Gironde, wine estates along the Rhône, Loire, and Rhine rivers, the great port vineyards of the Douro. So why not the Exe estuary? Their climate is mild and the success of other local vineyards has convinced me that it will be possible to produce outstanding wines here."

However, they can confidently say that Michael's dream of enjoying a flûte of his own Lympstone Manor Cuvée from grapes grown overlooking the beautiful Exe estuary is getting closer than ever.

## LYMPSTONE MANOR

Lympstone Manor above all is the vision of Michael Caines MBE and a realisation of a long-awaited dream. Through his inspiration and drive, the Grade II listed Georgian manor house has been imaginatively restored into a luxury country house hotel for the 21st Century, situated in the heart of Devon on the foreshore of the tranquil Exe Estuary. The hotel is set within 28 acres and has 21 individually designed bedrooms and suites, accompanied by a fine dining restaurant serving Michael's renowned cuisine. The hotel opened in April 2017, within six months Lympstone Manor was awarded a Michelin star and became a proud member of Relais and Châteaux.

## MICHAEL CAINES MBE

Lympstone Manor is Michael Caines' flagship hotel and restaurant overlooking the Exe Estuary in Devon, and forms part of the Michael Caines Collection alongside beachside restaurant and

bar, The Cove at Maenporth and The Harbourside Refuge in Porthleven. A fourth site, Mickeys Beach, is located in Exmouth seafront, looking down the coast to Torbay, Berry Head and the English Channel. Michael is also a partner and ambassador to the Williams Formula 1 racing team creating signature menus over the Grand Prix calendar and invests much time into the Michael Caines Academy, identifying the next generation of hospitality stars.

## NEW LUXURY SHEPHERD HUTS

Following a remarkable summer, Lympstone Manor has welcomed six indulgent Shepherd Huts complete with outdoor 'Hikki' hot tubs, rolltop baths and walk-in showers, as well as a new tennis court. More recently Michael and the team have celebrated the excitement of Lympstone's first vineyard harvest and planning consent to build a pool and accompanying pool house. The Shepherd Huts are aptly named after the hotel's

wildlife residents: Hare's Rest, Otter Holt, Beehive, Hedgehog Row and Fox Den. Sunrise is best enjoyed from Hare's Rest and Otter Holt, both positioned around a newly formed pond at the southernmost point of land at Lympstone, with views sweeping across the vines looking up at the house and with decked terraces extending over the pond. Sunsets are best enjoyed from the three huts; Fox Den, Beehive and Hedgehog Row with views both across the Estuary and the vineyard. Each hut has a private decking area with outside seating to enable you to immerse yourselves in the beauty of this tranquil spot. Badger Set, Otter Holt, Hare's Rest and Hedgehog Row have outdoor bathtubs, while Beehive and Fox Den both have free-standing bathtubs indoors and wood-fired 'Hikki' hot tubs outside. Crafted by Blackdown Shepherd Huts and complemented by Rachel Toll's hand-painted artwork, each cabin comprises of two braces and houses a kitchenette and lounge area. Each hut has a king-size bed with additional sleeping areas that have been engineered to disappear into the fabric of the hut so that each cabin will sleep between 4–5 guests, both adults and children. Breakfast hampers will be delivered each morning which include all the continental delights with cooked breakfast available in the main restaurant. The perfect place to unwind 'aprèsbeach' while 'staycationing' at Lympstone Manor.

## VISITING AND BUYING

General Enquiries
info@lympstonemanor.co.uk
Telephone: 01395 202040
Room Reservations
reservations@lympstonemanor.co.uk
Telephone: 01395 202040
Table Reservations
tables@lympstonemanor.co.uk
Telephone: 01395 200920

# MELBURY VALE

## DORSET

MELBURY VALE VINEYARD, FOOTS HILL, CANN, SHAFTESBURY, DORSET SP7 0BW

Melbury Vale

- 0.8 Ha **under vine**

- **Winemaker Clare Pestell**

- **Grape varieties Seyval Blanc, Pinot Noir, Solaris and Rondo**

### TERROIR

Perched on Foots Hill, which is of clay and greensand geology, Melbury Vale Vineyard is a family-owned, rural business specialising in the production of wines, liqueurs, brandies and ciders.

### ABOUT

Melbury Vale was bought in December 2003, by brother and sister, Glynn and Clare, as 28 acres of derelict and dilapidated farmland and buildings, formerly part of Barfoot Farm, near to Melbury Mill and Cann Mill.

They have lovingly converted the buildings and restored the land to good management with much determination, hard work, help and support from friends and family, to make it the varied and thriving rural business that it is today.

The on-site winery was completed and in production for 2013. It is built into the hillside with a number of sustainable design features, including a wild flower meadow turf roof as well as passive heating and cooling, combined with air source heat pump and rain water harvesting. Inquiries for new vineyards to be planted in the area came rolling in, with over 5,000 new vines already planted locally in response to the winery appearing in recent years. The winery has subsequently evolved into a small cooperative and contract wine-maker for Dorset based vineyards that do not have their own winery, bringing a diverse range of grape varieties to work with to produce the best, low intervention, still and sparkling wines.

Melbury Vale now also distills its own wine and makes liqueurs, brandy and aromatised wines, which are cocktails in a bottle all ready to drink!

## THE WINE

### Grace
A single variety, single vineyard wine that is produced in very limited quantities. On site at Melbury Vale Vineyard they have 500 established Seyval Blanc vines. Seyval Blanc as a grape is ideal for the Dorset climate in that it is low maintenance and ripens beautifully. Come harvest, the bunches of grapes are large and have sugar levels perfectly aligned for producing traditional method sparkling wine. This wine is a pale golden colour with fine bubbles typical of a high-quality English Sparkling Wine. On the nose there are aromas of fresh citrus and ripe pear, and on the palate there are notes of green apple, elderflower and lemon.

### Decadence
A blend of Seyval Blanc and Pinot Noir. On site at Melbury Vale Vineyard they have one block of established Seyval Blanc vines and one block of established Pinot Noir vines. While Pinot Noir is traditionally used in sparkling wine, Seyval Blanc has become a go-to English preference for sparkling production. Pinot Noir and Seyval Blanc at Melbury Vale ripen about the same time and are checked for sugar levels that are ideal for sparkling. This wine is a pale coral pink colour with fine bubbles typical of a high-quality English Sparkling Wine. On the nose there are aromas of fresh summer berries and meadow flowers, and on the palate there are notes of ripe strawberry, watermelon, and lime zest.

## VISITING AND BUYING
Visit their winery shop Fridays and Saturdays 10:00am to 4:00pm. Buy tours and wine online at
**mvwinery.co.uk**
**Clare Pestell**
**Email: info@mvwinery.co.uk**
**Telephone: 01747 854206**
**Mobile: 07730 955593**

# POLGOON VINEYARD AND ORCHARD

## CORNWALL

POLGOON VINEYARD ROSEHILL, PENZANCE, CORNWALL TR20 8TE

- 4.2 Ha **of planted vines**

- 1,500 to 3,000 **bottles depending on the season**

- **Winemaker** John Coulson

- **Vintage information** currently released 2018 still wines, 2016 sparkling

- **Grape varieties** Bacchus , Pinot Noir Precoce, Pinot Noir, Sauvignon Blanc, Ortega, Seyval Blanc, Rondo

## TERROIR

The fields are split into the old vineyard, planted in 2004, and the new, planted in 2005, and a third top field of Sauvignon Blanc planted in 2014. The aspect is sloping to south / south east and a mile inland from Mount's Bay. Based on granite base with a sandy soil, the slopes are quite free draining which is good considering the high rainfall in Cornwall. They have early spring warmth and little frost which is good for early season growth and then finishing the crop in September which has proved to be a good month for getting the ripeness needed for good wine. They are the first vineyard to grow vines in the UK under poly tunnels, which helps to reduce disease, pressure from all the rain, especially in Cornwall, and helps with improved fruit set and ripeness.

## ABOUT

Polgoon Farm was bought by John and Kim Coulson in 2002. Changing their careers from fishing to farming they turned the derelict flower farm into a home and an award-winning vineyard. The first wine produced was a still Rosé which scooped the award for the best still Rosé in the UK, which was followed by further accolades. This artisan vineyard is now the epitome of 'boutique'. Small bottling runs means that their wine is available in local outlets and restaurants only and they have a strong online presence.

## THE WINE

Polgoon wines are generally made from grapes grown on site at Polgoon Vineyard. They produce three White wines, Rosé wine, and their wine collection is topped by two sparklings, a single estate single variety pale Rosé Pinot Noir and a single estate crisp and citrusy Seyval Blanc. Both are made in the method traditional and are worthy of any celebration. Both are vegan friendly.

### 2016 PINOT NOIR SPARKLING ROSÉ

A single variety, single estate, excellent sparkling Rosé from Polgoon. A delicate pink colour and a golden hue, with a nose of zesty citrus and toasted crumb. A delicate palate with hints of tangerine, honey and spice. Hand harvest and whole berry pressed before being fermented until dry. Matured over the winter until bottled for secondary fermentation in the bottle.

### 2016 SEYVAL BLANC SPARKLING WHITE

A single variety, single estate, rather special sparkling from Polgoon. A flirt with green pear on the nose followed by delicate citrus notes and a good balanced acidity. Crisp and lively on the palate with a persistent mousse. Hand harvest and whole berry pressed before being fermented until dry.

Matured over the winter until bottled for secondary fermentation in the bottle.

## VISITING AND BUYING

Open 7 days a week Easter to Christmas, 6 days/ week out of season with tours most days, guided and self-guided.

Book in advance through tours@polgoon.com or the website www.polgoon.com

# Spotlight on
# SANDRIDGE BARTON WINES

## DEVON

SANDRIDGE BARTON WINES, LOWER WELL FARM, STOKE GABRIEL, DEVON TQ9 7UT

Sandridge Barton
The home of Sharpham Wine

- **14 Ha** of planted vines
- **70,000** bottles annually average
- **Winemaker** Duncan Schwab
- **Grape varieties** Madeleine Angevine, Pinot Noir, Bacchus, Pinot Gris, Chardonnay, Pinot Noir Précoce, and Pinot Blanc

## TERROIR

Sandridge Barton's vineyard sits on the banks of the river Dart in south Devon and benefits from a south facing aspect and shelter in the valley from predominant winds. The river is saltwater which helps to moderate the air temperature and is extremely tidal which can help with airflow. At a high tide the sun reflects on the vines focusing more energy to ripen the fruit. The soil is sandy loam with a rare (for the region) limestone ridge. In spring 2022 they will be planting another 7 acres as they begin to wind down the original Sharpham vineyard.

## ABOUT

The historic Sharpham site was originally planted by Maurice Ash in 1981 then extended at different periods up until 2008 when the larger Sandridge Barton vineyard was planted just 3 km (1.9 miles) down river. Predominantly a still wine producer championing the early ripening Madeleine Angevine and winning international awards on many occasions. As the industry has developed so too have the wines of Sandridge Barton and they now produce up to three traditional method sparkling wines championing Pinot Noir and Chardonnay as well as a skin contact Pinot Gris and a Red Pinot Noir thanks to the longer and milder growing season in the south west. They have just completed building their brand-new carbon neutral winery at their Sandridge Barton vineyard site, which will be the new home of their business from 2022.

## THE WINE

Sandridge Barton produce a few different styles but in smaller volumes in order to ensure that the wines are very different in style and promoting each variety. As well as their sparkling wines they also produce styles that range from dry to off-dry, oak matured to skin contact, Rosé wines and a Red Pinot Noir.

**Sparkling Blanc 2017 Pinot Noir / Chardonnay**
Classic and full-flavoured with yellow citrus, green apple and baked bread aromas. A richer palate of toast and lemon curd with great acidity. On lees for

30 months and finished with a 4.9 g/l dosage.

### Sparkling Reserve NV Pinot Noir / Chardonnay / Pinot Blanc

Rich and complex with baked apple, crème fraiche and white truffle. Another dry extra brut style but layered with toasted brioche, apple strudel and spice with a lifting saline finish. This NV blend is made with fruit from 2011 and 2012 that is matured in stainless steel before being bottled and matured for 70 months on the lees. Finished off with a 5 g/l dosage.

## VISITING AND BUYING

Wine available at www.sandridgebarton.com. Please check website for opening times and to book tours or tastings.
Email: info@sandridgebarton.com
Telephone: 01803 732203

# TREVIBBAN MILL VINEYARD & ORCHARDS

## CORNWALL

TREVIBBAN MILL VINEYARD & ORCHARDS, DARK LANE, NR PADSTOW, CORNWALL. PL27 7SE

- **4.8 Ha** planted vines and apple trees

- **30,000** bottles annually

- **Winemakers** Founders Engin and Liz Mumcuoglu, Consultant Winemaker Salvatore Leone

- **Vintage information** Producing vintage and non vintage wines annually

- **Grape varieties** Seyval Blanc, Reichensteiner, Pinot Noir, Pinot Noir Precoce, Dornfelder, Chardonnay, Bacchus

## TERROIR

The land slopes into the Issey Valley mostly facing South East. The soil is shillet (free draining sandy loam) full of slate with a little spa stone, and is very thin, only 30 cm (11.8 in) deep in places, sitting on solid slate. There is a disused slate quarry on site. The South Western climate is notoriously unpredictable, and so, each of the wines have character all of their own and without exception represent the quality of the vineyard and the work that goes into it; from pressing, fermenting and bottling, through to the disgorge and finishing processes of sparkling wine years later.

## ABOUT

Tucked away down a campion-lined Cornish lane, Trevibban Mill, is a family-run working vineyard, winery and events venue a stone's throw from the picturesque harbour town, Padstow. Historically the home of a miller and his family, the land is now the home to vines, apple trees and native English Southdown sheep. Engin and Liz Mumcuoglu established the vineyard in 2008 on a working arable farm with the vision to produce high quality sparkling and still wine on the coast of Cornwall. Everything from wine and cider making to bottling, disgorging and labelling are done on site, which gives greater control over quality. Today, Trevibban Mill is the leading edge of technology and innovation, continuously looking to improve quality as well as the range of wines and ciders produced.

## THE WINE

### Black Ewe Pink Sparkling

Deeply coloured aromatic pink sparkling wine bursting with flavour.
Aromas: fresh red berries, cranberry. Blend: 100% Dornfelder. Vintage: 2019. Size: 75cl. ABV: 12% Allergens: contains sulphites, vegan friendly.

### Pinot Noir, Pink Sparkling

Champagne & Sparkling Wine World Championship Silver Award.
Stylish Rosé sparkling wine with delicate fine bubbles. Aromas: strawberries and cream. Blend: 100% Pinot Noir. Vintage: 2014. Size: 75cl. ABV: 12%. Allergens: contains sulphites, vegan friendly.

### Black Ewe White Sparkling

A classic example of English Sparkling White, bone-dry and refreshing.
Aromas: green apple, lemon zest. On the palate: lemon sherbet, attractive fine bubbles. Blend: 100% Seyval Blanc. Vintage: 2018. Size: 75cl. ABV: 12%. Allergens: contains sulphites, vegan friendly

### Pet-Nat Sparkling

Unique sparkling White made with minimal intervention showcasing the vintage in all its glory.
Aromas: apricot, peaches, vanilla, honeydew melon. Blend: 100% Chardonnay. Vintage: 2020. Size: 75cl. ABV: 11% . Allergens: naturally occurring sulphites, vegan friendly.

### Blanc de Blancs

Decadent brut nature sparkling wine from an exceptional vintage. Aromas: biscuit, apple crumble, brioche. On the palate: pastry, crisp apple, savoury notes. Blend: 100% Chardonnay. Vintage: 2014. Size: 75cl. ABV: 12%. Allergens: contains sulphites, vegan friendly.

## VISITING AND BUYING

Vineyard Opening Hours
Wednesday – Sunday: 12–5 PM
Closed Monday–Tuesday
Please note: dogs are welcome, must be kept on a lead.
Buy online at www.trevibbanmill.com
Telephone: 01841 541413
E-mail: admin@trevibbanmill.com

# SOUTH CENTRAL

One of the first regions that started commercial wine production in England, South Central vineyards offer a terroir similar to that of the Champagne region, with mineral laden soils that contribute to refreshing wines with considerable lift.

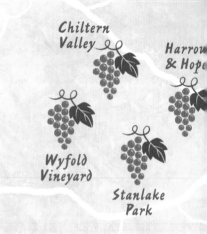

**Chafor Wine Estate**

**Chiltern Valley**

**Harrow & Hope**

**Wyfold Vineyard**

**Stanlake Park**

**Coates & Seely**

**Black Chalk Wine**

**Hattingley Valley Wines**

**Exton Park Vineyard**

**Leckford Estate**

**Hambledon Vineyard**

LONDON

# BLACK CHALK WINE

## HAMPSHIRE

BLACK CHALK WINE, FULLERTON ROAD SP11 7JX

- **12 Ha** of planted vines
- **30–40,000** bottles annually
- Winemaker **Jacob Leadley**
- Grape varieties **Chardonnay, Pinot Noir, Pinot Meunier**

## TERROIR

The Black Chalk vineyards lie in the heart of the beautiful Test Valley. Thirty acres of Hampshire chalk soil provide the foundation for 45,000 Chardonnay, Pinot Noir and Pinot Meunier vines. The vineyards are in a stunning setting with fantastic views. The River Test meanders its way around the site which not only helps to improve the views, but also attracts visitors from all over the world to fish for the famed River Test chalkstream trout.

## ABOUT

In 2009 Jacob Leadley left a comfortable job in London to retrain as a winemaker. He completed these studies and went on to work for 7 years as a winemaker at

another Hampshire winery. Over dinner with friends and family in 2015, talk turned to the idea of creating small production sparkling wine from locally sourced grapes and Black Chalk was born! Since then, it has become the family's passion, and has grown into a very successful company, they've acquired their own vineyards and built a state-of-the-art winery. The wines have been very well received, with the 2016 'Classic' winning 4 Gold Medals and 4 trophies.

## THE WINE

Black Chalk has been beautifully crafted by a family with their roots firmly planted in the chalklands of Southern England.

### Black Chalk Classic:
This small batch traditional method sparkling wine is created using the three classic varieties: Chardonnay, Pinot Noir and Pinot Meunier. The use of oak barrels and time on lees provide this wine with depth and complexity. The result is a fruit driven, perfectly balanced and crisp English Sparkling Wine.

### Black Chalk Wild Rose:
Pinot Noir, Pinot Meunier and Chardonnay combine

again to create their Wild Rose. A complex blend of rich, pure raspberries and strawberries that perfectly balance for a crisp, clean, very English finish.

## VISITING AND BUYING

**Website: www.blackchalkwine.co.uk**
**Telephone: 01264 860440**
**Socials: @blackchalkwine**

# CHAFOR WINE ESTATE

## BUCKINGHAMSHIRE

CHAFOR WINE ESTATE, HIGH HEDGES VINEYARD, PRESTON ROAD, GAWCOTT, BUCKS MK18 4HT

- **4.5 Ha** of planted vines
- **15,000** bottles annually
- **Winemaker** Tim Chafor
- **Vintage information** 2015 Cuvée and 2017 Rosé
- **Grape varieties** Chardonnay, Pinot Noir and Pinot Meunier

## TERROIR

Chafor Wine Estate is located in the heart of the English countryside in rural North Buckinghamshire. The estate's two vineyards are 16 miles apart with the home and larger vineyard at Gawcott and the second vineyard near Aylesbury.

**Gawcott:** Incredibly complex soils with a Jurassic Limestone base under a thin glacial deposit. Grading from smooth gravel riverbed pebbles on the west side to sharp, hard flinty sandy soil on the East side. The site aspect is due south with macro protection from the prevailing weather by the Cotswold Hills in the west and more closely a large forest on the South West boundary. In such a location the vines thrive and with such a favourable microclimate the Gawcott site consistently produces very clean grapes of optimum ripeness.

**Weedon:** Classic site, very sheltered and soil of Kimmeridgian origin. Vines nearly 20 years old with deep root systems.

## ABOUT

Relaxed, friendly and family-run, Chafor is a multiple award-winning boutique wine estate set in the heart of rural Buckinghamshire.

As a popular visitor attraction (located close to the prestigious F1 Grand Prix circuit at Silverstone), the winery, with a hand-built tasting room, benefits from ample car parking and also offers a self-guided nature trail with a lake-side seating area, ideal for picnics and BBQs with all the family.

The vineyard is open to the public on selected days during the summer months and offers a full programme of guided tours and wine tasting events.

The backdrop of well-tended rows of vines makes Chafor Wine Estate an inspirational venue for private functions and corporate events with an authentic wood-fired pizza oven, giant paella, BBQ, bouncy castle, licenced bar and marquees available for private hire. Tim and his dedicated team pride themselves on creating truly personalised wine tastings and vineyard events

## THE WINE

### Vintage Cuvée

Their premium PDO (Protected Designation of Origin) English White Sparkling wine. Produced every year using their finest Pinot Noir, Pinot Meunier and Chardonnay. The grapes are hand harvested and pressed gently in their state-of-the-art wine press. Production is Traditional Method with the first fermentation in steel tanks and small oak barrels, bottled and the second fermentation in the bottle. The wine is then left for 3–5 years to develop and build complexity before release.

### Vintage Rosé

Their premium Pink PDO English Sparkling wine is produced only in exceptional years with super ripe fruit. Vintage Rosé is produced with Pinot Noir and Pinot Meunier grapes in the Traditional Method with a small amount of Estate Made Pinot Noir Red wine used to give a very subtle, elegant pale pink colour. Bottle ageing is between 2–5 years. In terms of professional feedback based on reviews and competition results Vintage Rosé

is their top of the range wine. UKVA (national Competition) GOLD and 91 Parker Points.

### Amora

High quality traditional method sparkling wine with contemporary and stylish branding slightly sweeter in style than their Vintage wines. Typically bottle aged for up to 2 years before release.

## VISITING AND BUYING

Weekends 11am–4pm.
Telephone: 07973 892427
www.chafor.co.uk
Email: info@chafor.co.uk
https://www.facebook.com/CHAFORwine/

# CHILTERN VALLEY
# WINERY & BREWERY

## OXFORDSHIRE

CHILTERN VALLEY WINERY & BREWERY, OLD LUXTERS, HENLEY-ON-THAMES, RG9 6JW

- 1 Ha of planted vines
- 20,000 bottles annually
- Winemaker Donald Ealand
- Grape varieties Bacchus, Regent, Reichensteiner, Madeline Angevine

## TERROIR

Set in an area of outstanding natural beauty, Old Luxters is home to 'Chiltern Valley Wines', its vineyard, winery, Old Luxters brewery, liqueur making facilities and cellar shop. Their first vines were planted in 1982 on the slopes of the Chiltern Hills, surrounded by beech woodland and overlooking the beautiful Hambleden Valley near Henley-on-Thames, Oxfordshire, UK.

## ABOUT

Chiltern Valley are a business passionately committed to providing products which are uniquely hand crafted to the highest standards, linked with a service which is friendly and informed. Their modern production, bottling and labelling facilities, cellar shop and wine vats are all housed in traditional farm buildings. Since their first harvest in 1984, they have produced an increasing range of fine, award winning English wines to delight the eye and excite the palate. With scores of awards and commendations in blind-tasted national and international competitions, their wines have gained an enviable reputation for quality both here and abroad.

## THE WINE

They have used the very latest wine making techniques and equipment to combine a respect for tradition with minimum interference with the natural processes.

### English Sparkling Rosé

Grape variety: Pinot Noir. A crisp, dry sparkling Rosé with an elegant fizz created using traditional methods, including secondary fermentation in the bottle prior to 18 months of ageing on the lees. This wine has a wonderfully smooth effervescence and brings a delicate sweetness to the palate, a truly delicious experience.

### English Sparkling Wine

Grape variety: Madeline Angevine and Seyval | 2017 Vintage blend. This is a crisp, dry sparkling wine, created using traditional methods, including secondary fermentation in the bottle prior to 18 months of bottle ageing on the lees. The gentle bubbles creates a delicate yet delicious dry Champagne style wine.

## VISITING AND BUYING

Buy online at www.chilternvalley.co.uk
Telephone: 01491 638330
Email at: enquiries@chilternvalley.co.uk

# COATES AND SEELY

## HAMPSHIRE

COATES & SEELY, HARROWAY, WHITCHURCH (HANTS), RG28 7QT

## TERROIR

A mile to the south of Coates & Seely's vineyards, on the slopes of the North Hampshire Downs, the clear chalk stream of the River Test flows along the valley floor. On the vineyards, chalk soils and clay caps disgorge rugged flints that retain the heat of the sun, warming the top-soils, while in the late summer and early autumn the enclosed valley helps trap the last of the season's heat to ripen the grapes. The fruit that then emerges contains the perfect balance of crisp acidity and beguiling sweetness, as well as the saline minerality, that lie at the heart of all great sparkling wine.

## ABOUT

In 2008, two old friends Nicholas Coates and Christian Seely embarked on a quest. They had between them successful careers in finance and winemaking, an unshakeable belief, and a burning desire to make, one day, a sparkling wine to rival the best in the world. Their adventure drew them to the ancient chalk downlands of Hampshire, in southern England, to a secluded valley nestling quietly in the hills.

A decade later, their sparkling wines are listed in five royal palaces, Michelin-starred restaurants and iconic houses around the world, and have

- **12,0000** Ha of planted vines
- **70,000** bottles annually
- **Winemakers** Nicholas Coates and Christian Seely
- **Vintage information** Blanc de Blancs 2009 Vintage 'La Perfide'
- **Grape varieties** Pinot Noir, Pinot Meunier, Chardonnay

won Trophies and Gold Medals in all of the world's leading International wine competitions.

In 2019 their Blanc de Blancs 2009 'La Perfide' won the IWSC international trophy for 'Best Bottle Fermented Sparkling Wine', and in 2017 their wines won a clean sweep of the UK Wine Awards, winning the Supreme Champion Trophy along with the Trophies for the Best Sparkling Wine, The Best Rosé Sparkling Wine and the Best Blanc de Blancs Sparkling Wine.They are still the only English Sparkling Wine to be listed at the George V in Paris.

## THE WINE

### Brut Reserve NV
A blend of Chardonnay, Pinot Noir and Pinot Meunier, with reserve wines from previous years to create added complexity and consistency. Lees ageing is typically 30–36 months, with a further 6–12 months on cork to create a balance of freshness and bottle age.

### Rosé NV
A delightfully pale, salmon pink, made wholly from Pinot Noir and Pinot Meunier grapes and typically lees aged for 24 to 30 months. Some reserve wines, but with the emphasis on elegance and lightness.

### Blanc de Blancs 2009 and 2015 Vintage 'La Perfide'
100% Chardonnay and lees aged for a minimum of 5 years. The 2009 Blanc de Blancs has now won Trophies and Gold Medals in all of the leading international wine competitions and is on tight

allocation. The 2015 Blanc de Blancs 'La Perfide' is expected to release in 2022.

### Blanc de Noirs Vintage 2014 'La Perfide'
90% Pinot Noir and 10% Pinot Meunier, the first disgorgement of this vintage was on lees for 5 years and is being released at the time of writing. It was given the highest marks of any English Sparkling Wine in the most recent Robert Parker Wine Advocate review. Half of this wine remains on lees and will be disgorged for later releases.

### Rosé Vintage 2009 and 2014 'La Perfide'
Made wholly from Pinot Noir and Pinot Meunier grapes, each of the 2009 and 2014 Rosé vintages was 5 years on lees. The 2014 Rosé vintage is offered in magnum only and will be released in 2022.

### Brut Reserve Late Disgorgement
This is a select cuvée of 800 magnums of Brut Reserve NV, made from a blend of 2014, 2013 and 2011 wine (50% Pinot Noir, 10% Pinot Meunier and 40% Chardonnay). It was disgorged in 2020, having been on lees for nearly 6 years, with a further year on cork. It will be released in the second half of 2021.

## VISITING AND BUYING

Open by appointment.
General Enquiries:
Tel: 01256 892220
georgina.balmain@coatesandseely.com
Press Enquiries:
georgina.balmain@coatesandseely.com

# EXTON PARK

## HAMPSHIRE

EXTON PARK VINEYARD, ALLENS FARM LANE, EXTON, SOUTHAMPTON, HAMPSHIRE, SO32 3NW

- **24 Ha** of planted vines

- **63,000** bottles annually

- Winemaker **Corinne Seely**

- Reserve Blends **RB32 Brut, RB23 Rosé, RB28 Blanc de Noirs**

- Grape varieties **Pinot Noir, Chardonnay, Pinot Meunier**

## TERROIR

Exton Park is situated on a shoulder of land, off Beacon Hill in the South Downs National Park, Hampshire. The vines benefit from south, south-east and east facing aspects and range from 120 to 60 metres (394 to 197 ft) above sea level. The vineyard boasts a clay loam topsoil and a pure white middle chalk sub soil, offering a distinctive mineral flavour. The vines are dried by the south-west prevailing wind and exposed to the easterly sun, rising over Old Winchester Hill from the other side of the Meon Valley. The flavour of the grapes is influenced by a range of root stocks, clones, pruning systems, planting densities, a multitude of cover crops and plot-by-plot canopy management. This creates a unique and exciting terroir with hundreds of flavours captured in each wine.

## ABOUT

Reserve Blend is their signature style. The RB range draws on their 10 year library of reserve wines that they have curated and stored in their winery at Exton Park since 2011. Their winemaker, Corinne Seely, composes their blends from a huge variety of flavours captured from their single vineyard each year.

## THE WINE

### Exton Park RB23 Rosé

The refreshing and elegant RB23 Rosé is made with 70% Pinot Noir and 30% Pinot Meunier. The two black grape varieties are pressed slowly and gently to draw out the distinctive pale blush colour and an array of flavours. An average of 23 reserve wines are used in the blend with lees ageing for a minimum of three years. The result is a delicate, dry Rosé with a balanced floral character and complex notes of white peach and red berries. This is Exton Park's bestselling wine which has also been selected as the house pour by Michelin Star chef Simon Rogan.

### Exton Park RB32 Brut

Containing some of Exton Park's oldest reserve wines dating back to 2011, the RB32 Brut is an elegant expression that sings with subtle intrigue. It has been aged in bottle the longest out of all of the Reserve Blends and contains 60% Pinot Noir and 40% Chardonnay. Pale gold in colour, this wine harmonises 32 skilfully selected reserves which creates a generous nose with a bright lemony character and notes of passionfruit. Minerality in the mouth indicates a good, balanced structure with an intense backbone and a lengthy finish with a whisper of white pepper.

### Exton Park RB28 Blanc de Noirs

Made from 100% Pinot Noir from across Exton Park's single vineyard, the RB28 Blanc de Noirs is a truly stunning wine that never fails to impress. The expressive, fruity, lifted nose leads on to a rounded and balanced palate, showing tropical fruit, fresh dough and a touch of white pepper. Precise, charming, and English to its core with an average of 28 reserve wines in the blend. This is a limited production wine with only a small amount produced each year. With some of the top restaurants in the UK listing this wine, it has already become a firm favourite with foodies.

## VISITING AND BUYING

Visits by invitation only, please visit:
www.extonparkvineyard.com
General enquiries:
enquiries@extonparkvineyard.com
Telephone 01489 878788

# Spotlight on
# HARROW & HOPE

## BUCKINGHAMSHIRE

MARLOW WINERY, PUMP LANE NORTH, MARLOW SL7 3RD

HARROW & HOPE

MARLOW, ENGLAND

- **6.5 Ha** of planted vines
- **40,000** bottles annually
- **Winemaker** Henry Laithwaite
- **Grape varieties** Pinot Noir, Chardonnay, Pinot Meunier

## TERROIR

The 6.5 hectare (16 acre) vineyard is in one plot perched on the end of a Thames gravel terrace, formed by the river cutting into the Chilterns chalk around 450,000 years ago. It left behind a complex layer of clay, flint and gravel that is perfectly suited to Pinot Noir, giving it ripeness, texture and weight. Further down the slope the clay layer gets thinner before you get to the pure chalk that is home to their Chardonnay and Pinot Meunier. This gives freshness and minerality to the Chardonnay while keeping the Meunier elegant and aromatic with good acidity. The whole site is farmed organically with certification expected in 2023.

## ABOUT

The vineyard was founded by Henry and Kaye Laithwaite in 2010 after returning from Bordeaux where they also own 4 hectares (10 acres) of vines. Determined to set up in the Thames Valley and showcase what the unique 'Thames Terroir' has to offer, they got lucky when they found a plot on the outskirts of the beautiful Thameside market town of Marlow. They planted 35,000 vines at high density and built a winery in time for their first harvest in 2013. With expert help from Mike Roberts OBE and the Roberts family of Ridgeview and Dr Tony Jordon, ex Moet & Chandon and pioneering Australian sparkling winemaker, they had all the elements to get off to a flying start.

After numerous Gold Medals, trophies and winning UK Winery of the Year in 2019 the site has proved it's worth. Now working organically, they hope to push further in their quest to produce world class, single vineyard sparkling wines.

## THE WINE

### Brut Reserve NV No5

As they welcome No 5, they were overjoyed that in its last outing in the competitions No 4 won the NV English Sparkling Wine Trophy at the International Wine Challenge. Being based on 2016 it was the only wine they made that year as they lost 65% of their crop to frost. It turned out to be a great year but they simply didn't have the volume to make any other wines. It shows real elegance and freshness on release and the 20% barrel aged reserves really add those extra textural elements that give it their signature structure and weight.

This has the potential to be a very long-lived NV and maybe even eclipse its predecessor.

### Vintage Brut Rosé 2018

Their 5th vintage release of their ever-popular Rosé, this time from the truly exceptional year of 2018. The hottest and driest growing season for the last 30 years produced a ripe, abundant and disease-free crop; the rare trifecta in grape growing terms. This weather translated into an easy life for a winemaker, pick when you want, and then just gently guide the wine through the process without having to do much at all. As a consequence, you have an 'easy' wine, easy to make and consequently really easy to love. This 50% Pinot Noir, 35% Chardonnay, 10% Pinot Meunier blend receives a 7% Red Pinot Noir addition to add rich Red fruits, and a beautiful colour. They ferment 30% in aged oak barrels to build that lovely signature texture and weight. Open and friendly on release it will continue to develop more complexity for many years to come.

### Blanc de Noirs 2015

This wine epitomises everything that was great about 2015. A fantastic year for Pinot, the cool, dry and long season really helped to bring out the ethereal flavours of this famously finicky variety. They've certainly been patient, giving it 40 months

ageing on lees to really nurture these flavours and build texture and balance, giving the wine everything it needs for a very long life ahead. Although the 2015 is much more approachable at this stage than the 2013, don't be fooled. By all means have a bottle this Christmas, but it will only really start opening up around the middle of 2022. Time is the greatest winemaking tool.

## VISITING AND BUYING

Tours and visits all welcome by appointment only.
Telephone: **01628 481091**
Email: enquiries@harrowandhope.com

# HAMBLEDON VINEYARD

## HAMPSHIRE

HAMBLEDON VINEYARD, EAST STREET, HAMBLEDON, HAMPSHIRE PO7 4RY

- 85 Ha **of planted vines**
- 100,000 **bottles annually**
- Head winemaker **Hervé Jestin**
- Resident Winemaker **Felix Gabillet**
- Grape varieties **Chardonnay, Pinot Noir, Meunier**

### TERROIR

Geology has played a key role in the planning for Hambledon Vineyard. The chalk on which they grow their vines was formed on the seabed of the Paris basin some 65 million years ago. It is part of the Newhaven Chalk formation that developed between the Santonian and Campanian eras of the Upper Cretaceous period (known as the Senonian period in Champagne). The same chalk, with the same Belemnite content, is found in the best Chardonnay areas of the Côtes des Blancs in Champagne and is thought to be a key factor in the quality of the wines. Chalk is the perfect subsoil for growing vines because it acts like a sponge, retaining water when needed but also providing great drainage when it rains so that the vines do not get 'cold, wet feet!'

### ABOUT

As the oldest commercial vineyard in England, Hambledon is steeped in historical importance, with the eponymous village renowned as the 'cradle of cricket'. Major General Sir Guy Salisbury-Jones first established the vineyard back in 1952 with the help of the Pol Roger family, and at this time, the estate produced dry, still wines. Much later in 1999, Ian Kellett acquired Hambledon Vineyard and as a passionate wine lover, he was intrigued by the winemaking heritage of the property. After analysing the commercial potential for English wine, he began studying oenology at Plumpton College in Sussex with a view to restoring Hambledon to its former glory. Following essential soil and climate analysis, Ian decided to replant with the three grape varieties most commonly found in the Champagne region Chardonnay, Pinot Noir and Pinot Meunier. Today, Hambledon makes approximately 100,000 bottles of NV English Sparkling wine a year in the traditional method from 25 hectares (62 acres) of mature vines on pure chalk.

## THE WINE

The vision at Hambledon is to produce the best multi-vintage sparkling wine in England that will make Hambledon and the local community proud and gain universal recognition from the global wine community. They believe that there are two crucial elements to producing fine sparkling wines: using the best possible raw materials and working with the best winemakers in the business. Head winemaker Hervé Jestin has overseen the production of more than 200 million bottles of Champagne and sparkling wine during his career and was chef des caves at Champagne Duval Leroy for over 20 years. Hervé was originally recommended by Hubert de Billy, a director of Pol Roger, and is widely considered to be one of the best winemakers in the Champagne region. Since 2015, Felix Gabillet has been the full-time winemaker on site. A graduate of Changins University in Switzerland, Felix manages the winery on a day-to-day basis under Hervé's watchful eye. The on-site winery opened in time for its first harvest in 2011 and was subsequently opened officially by HRH Duchess of Cornwall. This state-of-the-art facility is the only fully gravity fed winery in the UK, allowing them to make wines with the minimal possible intervention.

### Hambledon Classic Cuvée

'Creamy, with elegant green apple fruit and some nice nutty development. The high acidity provides freshness, and there is some complexity on the quite round palate. There is a lovely vibrancy and great length of finish.' Christelle Guibert, *Decanter.*

### Hambledon Première Cuvée

'A standard-bearer for the quality that England can achieve. It's a very assured wine, with a firm acidic spine, but also has complexity and detail. Great focus and precision.' Victoria Moore, *The Telegraph.*

### Hambledon Classic Rosé Cuvée

'Crisp on the entry with a lovely chalky texture, saline and vibrant with a precise finish. This is the top English sparkling fizz from Hambledon that should drink well for several years.' Neal Martin, *Wine Advocate.*

### Hambledon Première Cuvée Rosé

The latest release from England's oldest vineyard – made from hand-picked, estate-grown Meunier grapes. A testament to the quality Meunier can achieve in Hampshire's chalky soils.

## VISITING AND BUYING

Monday – Saturday: 10:00 16:00. Sunday: By appointment.
Purchasing available at the tasting room/cellar door.

# *Spotlight on*
# HATTINGLEY VALLEY WINES

## HAMPSHIRE

HATTINGLEY VALLEY WINES, WIELD YARD, LOWER WIELD, NR ALRESFORD, HAMPSHIRE, SO24 9AJ

HATTINGLEY VALLEY

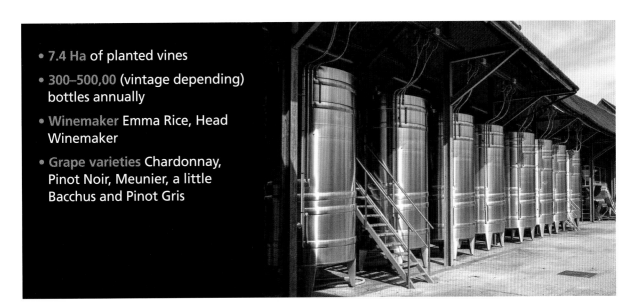

- **7.4 Ha** of planted vines
- **300–500,00** (vintage depending) bottles annually
- **Winemaker** Emma Rice, Head Winemaker
- **Grape varieties** Chardonnay, Pinot Noir, Meunier, a little Bacchus and Pinot Gris

## TERROIR

Hattingley sits on the western edge of the South Downs National Park, a geological phenomenon most romantically and obviously visualised by the White cliffs at Beachy Head in Sussex. In Hampshire the chalk bedrock is less visible but is actually where the largest concentration is found. Just a few centimetres below the flinty loam surface, the chalk acts as a giant sponge for the vines. It sucks the water from the surface avoiding waterlogging and yet holds the water just where the roots of the vines can access it when needed. Their slightly cooler climate, being inland and more exposed to the prevailing weather from the southwest, allows their vines a very long growing season. This slow, cool development of ripeness results in an unrivalled intensity of fruit flavours while maintaining low sugars and a perfect acidity for classic method sparkling wine.

## ABOUT

Family-owned Hattingley Valley, established in 2008 by owner Simon Robinson, specialises in premium, award-winning English Sparkling Wine. The Hattingley Valley winemaking team is headed up by Plumpton-trained Emma Rice who is twice winner of Winemaker of the Year in 2014 and 2016. With over 10 hectares (25 acres) of vines across two well-situated sites, as well as a full wine analysis laboratory on site, the eco-friendly vineyard is known for its refreshingly modern and innovative approach to winemaking. All wines are vegetarian and vegan friendly.

## THE WINE

### CLASSIC RESERVE NV

Their Classic Reserve is pale gold in colour with delicate and fine long-lasting bubbles. The beautifully complex bouquet combines aromas of green apples with creamy nougat, freshly baked

brioche and delicate toasted notes from ageing in the bottle. On the palate, the complexity continues with notes of soft lemon sherbet, biscuit and a subtle oak character. Refreshing and perfectly balanced, with a delightfully long finish.

### SPARKLING ROSÉ 2018

This elegant Rosé has a subtle delicate salmon hue and a soft mousse, with bright Red fruit and summer berry aromas. On the palate, experience delicious strawberry coulis flavours, creamy texture and fine toasty notes. A harmonious wine, with extraordinary depth, freshness and perfectly balanced acidity.

### KINGS CUVÉE 2014

With an attractive pale golden colour and fine mousse, their Kings Cuvée has vibrant citrus zest aromas layered with honey and nuts, all smoothly integrated with creamy oak, baked apples and marzipan. Deep and rich, yet refreshing on the palate with bright, crisp acidity and a long, complex finish. They make this every year if the weather

permits and this vintage has won the accolade of 'Supreme Champion' at the WineGB awards in 2020.

## VISITING AND BUYING

**Wines available at www.hattingleyvalley.co.uk**
Cellar door open 8:30am – 5pm Monday to Friday.
**Tours can be booked through their website or call them on 01256 389188.**
**Email: office@hattingleyvalley.co.uk**
**Telephone: 01256 389188**

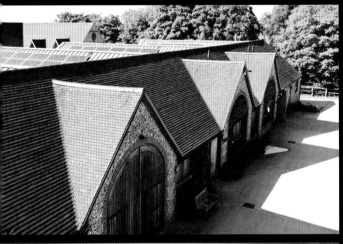

# *Spotlight on*
# LECKFORD ESTATE VINEYARDS

## HAMPSHIRE

LECKFORD ESTATE, THE WAITROSE FARM, LECKFORD, STOCKBRIDGE, HAMPSHIRE SO20 6DA

THE
WAITROSE & PARTNERS
FARM
—
LECKFORD ESTATE
EST. 1929

- **7 Ha** of planted vines
- **40,000** bottles expected annually
- **Winemaker** Simon Roberts, Ridgeview Winery
- **Vintage information** (available during 2021) Leckford Estate Brut 2016 and 2017
- **Grape varieties** Chardonnay, Pinot Noir and Pinot Meunier

## TERROIR

The Leckford Estate vineyards are located in the Test Valley, 3 kilometres (1.8 miles) north of Stockbridge and 300–900 metres (984–2,952 feet) east of the River Test. The two vineyards were planted in 2009 (4.7 hectares) and 2017 (2.3 hectares), the second one being immediately adjacent to the first. The soils across the two vineyards are classified within the Andover 1 soil association – shallow, well-drained, calcareous silty soils over chalk.

The near 25,000 vines are planted on 2.25 metre (7.3 feet) inter-row and 1.20 metre (4 ft) inter-vine intervals, on three different rootstocks appropriate to the terroir. The row orientation is along the south-west to north-east line, the lowest point being at 50 metres (164 ft) above-sea-level and the highest at 76 m (249 ft) asl. The aspect provides optimum conditions for growth and ripening, and the significant slope helps provide some natural frost protection.

The alleyways between the rows were established from 'natural regeneration', providing a diversity of native flora and protecting the soil from erosion.

## ABOUT

The John Lewis Partnership's 2,800-acre (1133 Ha) Leckford Estate in Hampshire was purchased by

the founder of the Partnership, John Spedan Lewis in 1929, and was the family home until he passed away in 1963. Since 2001, the estate has been known as The Waitrose Farm, and it remains the

73

only 'supermarket-owned' farm in the UK (www.leckfordestate.co.uk).

The people who work on the estate are all Partners in the UK's largest employee-owned company. One of these Partners, Colin Pratt, manages the two vineyards alongside several apple and pear orchards. Other farming activities include arable, beef and mushroom growing, supplying, amongst other things, Leckford-branded mushrooms, bread-flour and cold-pressed rapeseed oil into Waitrose & Partners stores. Other estate activities extend into retail and leisure, including fishing and golf.

Leckford Estate has been LEAF-Marque certified since 2001, so the farm has a long history of farming in an environmentally-responsible way. Indeed, more than 25% of the land area of the estate is managed primarily for environmental (conservation) objectives.

## THE WINE

### Leckford Estate Brut 2015

48% Chardonnay, 41% Pinot Noir, 11% Pinot Meunier

**Leckford Estate Brut 2016**
49% Chardonnay, 33% Pinot Noir, 18% Pinot Meunier

**Leckford Estate Blanc de Blanc 2014**
100% Chardonnay

## VISITING AND BUYING

Their sparkling wine is available in selected Waitrose & Partners stores and on Waitrose Cellar (www.waitrosecellar.com). The vineyards are generally not open for tours, although farm tours can be arranged for larger groups. Customers are always welcome at their Farm Shop, Café and Plant Nursery (www.leckfordestate.co.uk/farm-shop-and-cafe). Their highly regarded Longstock Park Water Gardens are also open to the public (www.leckfordestate.co.uk/water-garden).

For all general enquiries, please contact their Estate Office:

Online:
www.leckfordestate.co.uk/estate-contact
Telephone: 01264 812110

# STANLAKE PARK
# WINE ESTATE

## BERKSHIRE

STANLAKE PARK, TWYFORD, READING, BERKSHIRE RG10 0BN

- 4 Ha **of planted vines**

- **25,000** bottles annually

- **Winemaker Nico Centonze**

- **Grape varieties Chardonnay, Pinot Noir, Meunier, Seyval Blanc**

## TERROIR

There are a number of sites, mainly south-east facing and between 40 m (131 feet) and 70 m (229 feet) above sea level. The soils vary from sand to loam and clay.

The vines are planted on a variety of spacings and training systems, including some unique to the Estate such as the 'Stanlake Bow' and the 'Stanlake Ballerina', which is a variant of the Smart-Dyson Ballerina, in effect a mid-height Sylvoz system; this system is ideal for long cool growing seasons, giving the resultant fruit a perfect balance between quality and yield. Vines are between 20 and 40 years-old, and benefit from large bodies of permanent wood, earlier bud-burst which adds protection from spring frost.

Major grape varieties include Pinot Noir, Meunier, Chardonnay, Seyval Blanc, Bacchus, Gewurztraminer, Dornfelder, Schonburger and others.

## ABOUT

Since 1979 Stanlake Park Wine Estate has developed some of the highest quality vineyards in England, and produces a wide range of wines, including White, Rosé, Red and traditional method sparkling wine. Winemaking takes place within a 17th Century Reformation barn which houses the largest winery in Berkshire, capable of handling over 200 tonnes of fruit in any one season.

Nico Centonze, Stanlake Park's skilful Italian winemaker, personally follows the progress of each wine, carefully tasting, blending and selecting which wines to bottle or to mature. The whole wine making process, from vine to bottle, is meticulously overseen and guaranteed.

Stanlake Park also provides bespoke contract winemaking services, allowing local vineyards to enhance fruit expression through a minimal intervention – yet modern – approach.

The success of both their own wine and the wine made for other regional vineyards has led Stanlake Park to become one of the largest and best-known winemakers in Berkshire.

## THE WINE

### Heritage Brut NV:

A light, crisp sparkling wine with delicate floral notes and hints of lemon, green apple and toast. Elegant and refreshing, the Heritage Brut is made with Pinot Noir and Seyval Blanc grapes and aged for 12 months on the lees.

### Rosé Superior NV:

This delicate Rosé is made with 100% Pinot Noir grapes and aged for 24 months on the lees. The wine is light and refreshing, and shows delicate Red fruit notes such as raspberry and strawberry, and floral hints. Independent English Wine Awards IEWA, Silver Medal; International Wine Challenge IWC, Bronze Medal; T&CVA Annual Wine Challenge, Bronze Medal.

### Stanlake Brut NV:

Their flagship sparkling wine is made mainly with Pinot Noir grapes, with a small percentage of Chardonnay. Having spent many years ageing on its lees, this elegant English Sparkling Wine has a bright lemon colour with golden hints and complex aromas and flavours of yellow apple, peach, biscuit and pastry. Creamy in the palate, with a lingering finish of yeasty notes.

## VISITING AND BUYING

Wine Bar & Gift Shop open Tuesday to Sunday. Vineyard Tours and Tastings available all year round.
General enquires:
Telephone: 0118 934 0176
Email: info@stanlakepark.com
Trade enquires: natalia@stanlakepark.com
Tours information: tours@stanlakepark.com
Website: www.stanlakepark.com

# Spotlight on
# WYFOLD VINEYARD

## OXFORDSHIRE

WYFOLD VINEYARD, WYFOLD LANE, WYFOLD, OXFORDSHIRE RG4 9HU

- **2.2 Ha** of planted vines
- **12–18,000** bottles annually
- **Winemaker** Henry Laithwaite at Harrow and Hope, Marlow
- **Grape varieties** Chardonnay, Pinot Noir, Pinot Meunier

## TERROIR

Wyfold is a small, stony, sunny, south-facing vineyard which sits on Thames gravel above chalk in the Chiltern Hills near Henley-on-Thames. It is relatively high, top rows at 120 m (390 ft), and starts the growing season a little later than most in the South of England. This is both an advantage as later bud burst helps to avoid some of the spring frost damage, and a disadvantage as they harvest later than others, sometimes well into autumn (though this can have advantages too!). It's open and sunny position gives optimum cool climate grape growing conditions and a gentle westerly breeze provides natural air conditioning to keep the vines healthy.

## ABOUT

Wyfold was planted in 2003 by Barbara Laithwaite and a friend. It was mentored by the late Mike Roberts of Ridgeview estate. It's a family affair; the Laithwaite family, fairly well known in wine circles, is involved with Barbara managing the vineyard, son Henry in charge of the winemaking, husband Tony and sons Tom and Will giving hands-on support in the vineyard. Its first commercial vintage, 2009, set the standard by winning Stephen Skelton's 'Judgement of Parsons Green' thereby beating most well-known English Sparkling Wines and several Champagnes. Barbara set her sights on maintaining this position, staying small and becoming the outstanding single grower sparkling wine in her region. Wyfold has won many awards and Gold Medals since.

Wyfold concentrates on soil management and plant nutrition. It's programme of winter and summer cover crops, organic compost applications and meticulous canopy management ensures the best results and the lowest possible use of fungicides. It tries hard to balance mechanical weed control with as few tractor passes as possible and has a programme of improving soil carbon levels over the years.

Barbara is very 'hands-on' in the vineyard and manages most of the manual work herself with the help of a shared vineyard manager from Windsor Great Park, contract workers and an enthusiastic band of volunteers who come from far and wide. Her aim is to grow the best sparkling wine grapes possible while allowing others to enjoy the

tranquility of a sunny vineyard and improving the soil as she goes along. The odd Gold Medal along the way is for encouragement!

## THE WINE

Since 2014 Wyfold has been producing a Brut and a Rosé each year. As the vineyard is planted with 50% Chardonnay, this is the grape variety that dominates and in more difficult years will provide more than 50% of the crop as the Pinots are more weather susceptible. The grapes are usually harvested in early October though early November has been known. The Pinots will ripen first and the Chardonnay a few days later. They are immediately transported in small baskets, to keep them undamaged, 10 miles to the Harrow and Hope winery in Marlow and pressed the same day.

This is all to preserve their freshness and prevent any type of oxidation contamination.

All wines are released as vintage wines and in recent years Wyfold has built up around 17 barrels (equivalent to over 5,000 bottles) of reserve wine which is used in the spring blending/bottling process and the disgorgement 'dosage'.

### Classic Sparkling Brut

Wyfold Brut's signature is it's vivid minerality drawn up from the Thames Terrace gravels and the chalk bedrock below. The Brut is bottle fermented by the 'Methode Traditionelle' like all the world's finest sparklers but for a year longer than most. As a minimum it has 3.5 years in bottle on the lees and another six months ageing after disgorgement. It is an elegant and classy wine

displaying crisp summer fruits notes and perfect for any celebration. It is usually released 5 years after harvest, for example the 2016 Brut will be released in the autumn of 2021.

### Classic Sparkling Rosé

Using the same meticulous winemaking as the Brut, Wyfold Rosé is pale salmon in colour with aromas of dark Red fruit and cherries. The textured palate is broad, soft and rounded with a strong Pinot character that drives the flavours to a long, lingering finish. As a minimum it has 2 years in bottle on the lees and another six months ageing after disgorgement. It is usually released 3.5 years after harvest, for example the 2017 Rosé will be released in spring 2021.

## VISITING AND BUYING

Visits to Wyfold are By Appointment. Please also contact if you are interested in joining the Friends of Wyfold volunteer groups or receiving the Spring, Summer and Autumn Newsletters.
Contact address: sales@wyfoldvineyard.com
Wine Sales are through
www.laithwaites.co.uk for national delivery, or sales@wyfoldvineyard.com for local collection. Also available in local pubs and restaurants.
www.wyfoldvineyard.com
Correspondence address: Barbara Laithwaite, The Chalet, Peppard Common, Henley on Thames, Oxfordshire RG9 5EH

Jenkyn Place

Denbies Wine Estate

Greyfriars

Albury Organic

Blackdown Ridge

Bolney
Wine
Estate

Ridgevi
Wine
Estat

Nyetimber

Roebuck
Vineyard

Wiston
Estate

Court
Garden

Ashling Park
Estate

Tinwood Estate

Digby

# SOUTH EAST

The UK's sunniest region, the South East contains the majority of commercial vineyards. 88 miles further north than Champagne, this region maybe cooler with a maritime climate but they have a longer flowering season which develops more complexity in the juice and is therefore why it is home to some of the most highly regarded Sparkling Wine producers.

# ALBURY ORGANIC VINEYARD

## SURREY

ALBURY ORGANIC VINEYARD, SILENT POOL, SHERE ROAD, ALBURY GU5 9BW

- 5 Ha **of planted vines**

- **20,000** bottles annually

- **Founder and Owner Nick Wenman**

- **Winemaker Matthieu Elzinger**

- **Grape varieties Pinot Noir, Chardonnay, Pinot Meunier, Seyval Blanc**

## TERROIR

Albury Vineyard is situated on the southern slopes of the North Downs near Guildford, in the beautiful Surrey Hills, an Area of Outstanding Natural Beauty. The soil is clay on chalk, similar to much of Champagne. They are committed to growing biodynamic fruit without the use of chemicals such as herbicides and fungicides, and produce organic wines of the highest quality.

## ABOUT

Albury Vineyard is the result of Nick Wenman's passion for quality wine. Nick planted the vineyard in 2009 having retired from the IT industry to fulfil his dream of owning a vineyard. Nick believes that the key to the success of the wines is the vineyard's commitment to organic and biodynamic principles, together with excellent winemakers and his talented vineyard manager Alex, one of the few female vineyard managers in England. Her expertise is vital to the running of the vineyard, and her dogs Attila and Ulysee are well loved by visitors. Albury is a family-run vineyard, with Nick's daughter Lucy now part of the team, and granddaughter Poppy a regular visitor (if only to visit the bee-hives and sneak a taste of the honey!)

### THE WINE

### Albury Estate Classic Cuvée
Made from a classic blend of biodynamic Pinot Noir, Pinot Meunier and Chardonnay grapes. It is an elegant dry English Sparkling Wine with subtle Red berry flavours and light citrus aromas, it consistently wins international gold awards.

### Albury Estate Blanc de Blancs
A blend of Chardonnay and Seyval Blanc. It is fresh, crisp and dry with a hint of honeyed sweetness and citrus and herb aromas.

### Albury Estate Prestige Cuvée
Only made from exceptionally good vintages, it is blended from the first pressing biodynamic Pinot Noir, Pinot Meunier and Chardonnay grapes. It is a very dry ultra brut wine that is aged in the bottle for at least 4 years.

### Albury Estate Biodynamic Wild Ferment
Very limited release, only made from 100% Chardonnay grapes, fermented using wild yeasts found naturally on the vineyard, giving the wine a unique sense of place or terroir.

### VISITING AND BUYING

Their wines can be tasted in a relaxed and informal environment at the vineyard. Everyone is welcome, regardless of how much or little you know about wine. Whether you pop in on a Saturday for a tasting, stay to enjoy a glass or two on their patio with one of their cheese platters, or stroll up the vineyard to take in the views, you will be sure to enjoy your visit. They also offer new self-guided vineyard tours. It's free to do, and a great way to find out a bit more about them. Families are welcome and they have a vineyard toy trail to entertain little ones.

**For more information visit www.alburyvineyard.com**

# ASHLING PARK ESTATE

## SUSSEX

ASHLING PARK ESTATE, FUNTINGTON, PO18 9DJ

- 12 Ha of planted vines

- 40 to 60k bottles annually

- Winemaker Dermot Sugrue

- Grape varieties Pinot Noir, Chardonnay, Pinot Meunier

## TERROIR

With two vineyards in the South Downs, Ashling Park have the perfect growing conditions to produce their trophy award winning wines.

The home vineyard has the distinctive South Downs chalk stones and flint signature. With the sea just 1.6 km (1 mile) away and the Downs on the doorstep, it really is a lovely warm spot, perfect for the grapes.

## ABOUT

This wonderful wine retreat brings you a new style of vineyard stay, with tours and tastings. So beautifully framed between the South Downs and the shoreline, it's a playground for the wine lover. The newly opened tasting room and luxurious lodges were designed and built by Will Hardie of Channel 4's *Amazing Spaces*. The tasting rooms boast an experience room, a shop, a gin school and incredible views for the seasonal dishes, cleverly designed around their wine, bees and gin.

Each overnight lodge is named to depict the cycle of the vineyard; Budburst, Flowering, Véraison, Harvest and Fall and are furnished to reflect the colour of the season. There's attention to detail for the ultimate opulence from the gold leaf roll-top bath, a baby wood burner and hand-painted walls in the heights of the apex bedroom.

## THE WINE

The prestigious wine competition Wine GB have just awarded Ashling Park the trophy for the Best Classic Cuvée NV in the UK for the second year running. This firmly puts Ashling Park on the global stage with the Sparkling Rosé also a previous trophy winner.

### Ashling Park Cuvée
Crisp and precise with impressive persistence and balance. Delicious for drinking now, but with terrific ageing potential.

### Ashling Park Sparkling Rosé
Elegant and full-flavoured with great intensity of fruit, length and complexity.

### Ashling Park Blanc de Blancs
An elegant nose of fresh citrus, brioche and white flowers, leading to a palate of lime, marzipan, almond and toasty notes.

They also have a range of delicious still wines all from the 2020 harvest – a Chardonnay, a Pinot Meunier Rosé, a Bacchus and a limited edition Pinot Noir.

## VISITING AND BUYING

Open Thursday to Sunday, booking advisable.
www.ashlingpark.co.uk
contact@ashlingpark.co.uk
tours@ashlingpark.co.uk

# BALFOUR WINERY

## KENT

BALFOUR WINERY, HUSH HEATH ESTATE, FIVE OAK LANE, STAPLEHURST, KENT, TN12 0HT

- 150,000 Ha **of planted vines**

- 300,000 **bottles annually**

- **Winemakers Owen and Fergus Elias**

- **Grape varieties Chardonnay, Pinot Noir, Pinot Meunier and Bacchus**

## TERROIR

Each of Balfour's vineyards has been carefully chosen and planted to complement their winemaking philosophy. Located on either clay, chalk or greensand each vineyard is an expression of its unique terroir.

Over half of their vineyards are on Hush Heath Estate. Planted on Wealden Clay, these sites produce many of their single vineyard wines, including their flagship Balfour Brut Rosé.

Vineyards planted on Greensand, known for wines of poise and balance and Chalk, showing wines with a lean, clean character, allow an opportunity to explore Kent's wonderful and varied terroir.

To allow greater diversity and complexity each vineyard was planted with multiple clones and rootstocks, each

### Balfour Brut Rosé

One of England's most recognisable wines and the first English wine chosen by British Airways.

A single-vineyard wine planted in 2002 with clones and rootstocks specifically chosen to make a world-class sparkling Rosé.

From vines on Wealden clay, the grapes are full of richness and intense flavour. To maximise this character the grapes are often the last to be picked on the Hush Heath Estate. To emphasise the purity of the fruit, Balfour Brut Rosé never undergoes malolactic fermentation. A wine of intense concentration that embraces precision and fresh English acidity.

### Leslie's Reserve Gold

Bridging the gap between Brut and Demi-Sec, Leslie's Reserve Gold is rich and ripe. A touch of sweetness works in harmony with the fresh English acidity to produce a wine of beautiful poise and balance. Red apple rather than green apple characters dominate. Rich and unctuous, with flavours of ripe black and Red fruits not often seen in traditional method sparkling wines. A wine that works beautifully as an aperitif but also with huge gastronomic potential.

**Les sixes**
**Saignée 2018**
**Victoria Ash Blanc de Blancs 2012/2013**
**Balfour Skye's Blanc de Blancs 2014**
**Balfour Brut Rosé 2017**
**Leslie's Reserve Brut, NV**
**Leslie's Reserve Rosé**
**Leslie's Reserve Gold, NV**
**Balfour Leslie's Reserve Red**

## VISITING AND BUYING

Balfour Winery is open year round for visits and runs events and tastings throughout the year. **Visit www.balfourwinery.com or call 01622 832794 for more details.**

chosen carefully by winemaker Owen Elias.

Every clone and variety in each vineyard is monitored separately so that each parcel is hand-picked only at optimal ripeness.

## ABOUT

Balfour winery is located on the 162 Ha (400 acre) Hush Heath Estate. Rich in flora and fauna it compromises 400 acres of manicured vineyards, apple orchards, wildflower meadows and ancient oak woodland. Sustainability and conservation are of paramount importance and is reflected in the practices used across the Estate.

Co-founders Richard and Leslie Balfour-Lynn planted their first vineyard on Hush Heath Estate in 2002, and when Balfour Brut Rosé 2004 became the first English wine to win a Trophy at the International Wine Challenge in 2007, Balfour was on the wine map. Now Balfour Winery is one of England's leading wine producers, pioneers for both English traditional method sparkling wines, and a new wave of English still wines.

# BIDDENDEN VINEYARDS

## KENT

GRIBBLE BRIDGE LANE, BIDDENDEN, TN27 8DF

- **9.3 Ha** of planted vines
- **80,000** bottles annually
- **Winemakers** Julian Barnes, Tom Barnes and Will Barnes
- **Grape varieties** Ortega, Pinot Noir, Reichensteiner and Scheurebe

## TERROIR

The single estate vineyards spans 9.3 ha (23 acres) of gentle south facing slopes, situated in a sheltered valley. The soil is sandy loam over clay, which combined with the situation of the vineyard creates perfect conditions for both Germanic and French grape varieties.

## ABOUT

Kent's original vineyard, Biddenden was established by the Barnes family in 1969. The vineyard has remained family owned and is today run by the second and third generation, drawing on many years of experience in winemaking at

Biddenden. Eleven varieties of grapes are grown across 23 acres, producing quality award-winning White, Red, Rosé and sparkling English wines. Ortega, Biddenden's signature variety accounts for approximately half of the vineyard.

Approximately 80,000 bottles of wine are produced each year and all of the grapes are estate grown, with all vine work and picking carried out by hand to ensure the best quality grapes are selected for Biddenden's wines. Pressing, fermentation and bottling is also carried out on site, the majority of wines are sold directly from the cellar door.

## THE WINE

### Sparkling Ortega Demi-Sec 2019

Floral to the nose and aromatic with sweet green apple undertones, with a fine stream of bubbles. Ortega was part of the original planting at Biddenden, now approaching 50 years in age and being some of the oldest vines in Kent. The 2019 harvest was earlier than usual owing to the long, hot summer which meant that picking of early ripening Ortega began on 12 September 2019. Specially selected grapes have been hand-picked and pressed on site to produce Biddenden Sparkling Ortega Demi-Sec. The rich, fruity varietal characteristics of these well-established wines shine through.

### Gribble Bridge Sparkling White 2016

Dry, intense and supple with fresh bready, baked notes. This is clean, fresh and has depth. Made by the traditional method with Pinot Noir, Reichensteiner and Scheurebe.

### Pinot Reserve 2015

A dry, fruity wine, rich and creamy with hints of brioche, good length and mousse.

Made by the traditional method with carefully selected and delicately pressed Pinot Noir.

### Gribble Bridge Sparkling Rosé 2017

Produced from Pinot Noir and Reichensteiner, an off-dry sparkling Rosé with blushing damask rose tones which come to life thanks to the inexhaustible stream of bubbles. The palate conjures up sweet summer fruit, think strawberry, raspberry and pear, with a half-squeeze of lemon.

## VISITING AND BUYING

Biddenden's full range may be bought online for nationwide home delivery at
www.biddendenvineyards.com
The vineyard shop is open throughout the year, for latest information on visiting, please see their website.

# BLACKDOWN RIDGE

## WEST SUSSEX

BLACKDOWN RIDGE ESTATE, LURGASHALL, WEST SUSSEX, GU27 3BT

*Blackdown Ridge*

- 10.5 Ha **of planted vines**

- 30,000 **bottles annually**

- Winemaker **Martin Cook**

- Grape varieties **Pinot Noir, Pinot Meunier and Chardonnay**

### TERROIR

Blackdown Ridge Estate sits at 134 m (440 feet) above sea level in the Sussex Weald, enjoying extraordinary views over the South Downs National Park.

Here they have planted vines to create fine English wines, taking advantage of the superb location and conditions. The soil of the Sussex Weald shares much with the terroir of the Champagne region of France, and this influenced their plantings of the classic sparkling wine varietals: Pinot Noir, Pinot Meunier and Chardonnay. The vines planted for their range of still wines include the aromatic Bacchus for their single varietal English White wine, Triomphe for their smooth and velvety Red wine, and more recently, Sauvignon Blanc.

## ABOUT

The wines of Blackdown Ridge Estate are the result of the vision of owner, Professor Martin Cook, who has lived on the estate for nearly 25 years. Having realised that the beautiful, serene south-facing slopes of Blackdown would be perfect for growing vines, Martin was inspired to realise the potential of the estate and the first vines were planted in 2010.

The vines are nurtured throughout the growing year with an environmentally sensitive approach to viticulture that ensures optimum ripeness, yield and fruit quality.

All the wines produced at Blackdown Ridge are made from their own grapes and processed in their purpose-built winery. They are matured in the bottle for at least 2 years before release. Before release their wines go through a system of independent testing and tasting, for quality and provenance, to obtain PGI (Protected Geographical Indication) or PDO (Product of Designated Origin) status.

From the very beginning, they have tried to follow a sustainable and minimalistic philosophy at Blackdown Ridge. To achieve this, they take a minimal intervention approach in both the vineyard and the winery. Blackdown Ridge Estate's purpose-built winery, with the capability to produce up to 30,000 bottles is ready for the 2021 harvest and production of their still and sparkling wines.

Each vintage allows them to learn and improve, so much so that they now are successful in both national and international competitions which allows them to measure themselves against the very best. They are very proud of what they have achieved in so little time, but they're also continually aiming to refine and exceed expectations.

Their distinctive feather branding was inspired by Goosetoff, the resident goose on their lake who has been here longer than the vines. The feather is a symbol of strength and protection but they also hope that it will represent the feeling of peace, harmony and tranquillity that they have achieved.

They are a small but cohesive team, and their ethos is to create superb wines, spread the word about the wonderful English wine industry, and encourage visitors to spend time in the wonderful countryside overlooking the South Downs National Park.

## THE WINE

### 2015 Traditional Method Sparkling Rosé

Made predominantly from Pinot Noir with a small amount of Pinot Meunier added for structure the wine displays a bright bouquet of strawberries and floral notes. The palate is crisp yet rich with Red berry fruit and White peach flavours.

### Primordia 2014

A classic blend of Chardonnay, Pinot Noir and Pinot Meunier made using the traditional method. The wine has a persistent lively perlage and characteristic aroma. Lively, fine bubbles help to distribute this wine's wonderful aromatics; lemon zest and fruity apricot notes with orchard fruit and hints of sweet pastry. On the palate is a really lively citrus quality that is more lemon sherbet than lemon zest, prompting a lovely tingling sensation. Richer fruity flavours continue on the mid, taste ripe apricot with juicy apple and pear. A fine mousse with those deliciously rounded fruit flavours make this a really enjoyable and smooth drinking sparkling wine, while that persistent sherbet lemon quality keeps it refreshing and light.

## VISITING AND BUYING

They look to welcoming you to safer parameters and warmer weather, for a few hours escapism. Enjoy the tranquillity and peacefulness and learn about the varieties and management of their vines throughout the year, the wine making process from vine to bottle, then taste their award-winning English wines.
Tours run from April to late November.
www.blackdownridge.co.uk/shop
Email admin@blackdownridge.co.uk
Telephone 01428 656003
Mobile 07908 989566

# BLUEBELL VINEYARD ESTATES

## EAST SUSSEX

GLENMORE FARM, SLIDERS LANE, FURNERS GREEN, EAST SUSSEX TN22 3RU

- 40 Ha **of planted vines**

- 120,000 **bottles annually**

- **Winemaker Kevin Sutherland**

- **Vintage information Range from 2013 to 2016**

- **Grape varieties Chardonnay, Pinot Noir, Merlot, Seyval and Pinot Meunier**

## TERROIR

Bluebell Vineyard Estates, established in 2005, have over 100 acres of planting, with 130,000 vines planted in their Sussex Estate. 85 per cent of the plantings are for sparkling wine, and they also have Bacchus, Ortega and Chassalas, all white grape varieties which are planted for still wines. They are the only current producer of estate grown Merlot in the UK which they use in their sparkling Red and still Rosé. They are in the Top Ten in terms of vineyard plantings in England and Wales, with all aspects of the production located on site.

## ABOUT

Set amidst bluebell-strewn woods from which the vineyard derives its name, Bluebell Vineyard Estates is a family-run vineyard and winery who live on site and run the business with a passion for producing world class still and sparkling wines. Established as a vineyard in 2005, they are on the site of Glenmore Farm, which used to be the biggest working pig farm in the area with up to 10,000 pigs at its peak. The owners bought the farm in 1982 and ran it as a pig farm, but the farm closed in the late 1980s and the land went fallow and the buildings derelict. By then English wine was beginning to take off and they saw an opportunity to put the land back into productive, agricultural use. Three fields were planted in 2005/2006 with Chardonnay, Pinot Noir and Pinot Meunier, and since then they have purchased two further sites. They have a 50 acre site on Ketches Lane (around the corner) and a further 40 acres a 10 minute drive away.

## THE WINE

Bluebell Vineyard Estates craft their wines using the traditional method of production and strive to produce wines with the perfect balance of fruit character, acidity and ageing. All Bluebell wines are vintage wines, that is to say they are made exclusively from grapes grown in a single year. This means that every Hindleap and Ashdown Vintage is unique. Since their first commercial release from the 2008 vintage their wines have gone on to critical acclaim.

### Classic Cuvée 2015
A Chardonnay-dominant blend, underpinned by the Red fruit characters of Pinot Noir and Pinot Meunier.

### Blanc de Blancs 2016
Their signature wine, only the finest Chardonnay grapes are selected for their Blanc de Blancs.

### Rosé 2015
The epitome of their fruit-forward style, only the most characterful Pinot Noir and Pinot Meunier base wines are selected for their Rosé.

### Seyval Blanc 2015
Made from 100% Seyval Blanc, this grape is perfectly suited to the English climate and the 2015 vintage has resulted in a sparkling wine that has aromas of green apple, pear and elderflower that give way to lime, orange and tropical fruits on the palate. Creating a wine with zesty acidity, rich mouthfeel and a lovely long finish.

### Barrel Aged Blanc de Blancs 2016
Produced from 100% Chardonnay this 2016 Blanc de Blancs has been aged in the barrel for six months giving it delicious honey and vanilla tones underpinned with citrus freshness.

### Hindleap Sparkling Ruby 2018
This sparkling Red is made from Merlot Grapes and has aromas of Red cherry, raspberry and spice which are met on the palate with a fine mousse and silky tannins, which pairs beautifully with cheese.

## VISITING AND BUYING

**Open 10am till 4pm Monday Saturday and 11am to 4pm on a Sunday**
**General and Press Enquiries**
**Email: wineinfo@bluebellvineyard.co.uk**
**Telephone: 01825 791561**

# Spotlight on
# BOLNEY WINE ESTATE

## SUSSEX

BOLNEY WINE ESTATE, FOXHOLE LANE, BOLNEY, HAYWARDS HEATH, RH17 5NB

- **15.5 Ha** of planted vines
- **250,000** bottles annually
- **Winemakers** Cara Lee Dely and Tom Sutton
- **Grape varieties** Pinot Noir, Rondo, Dornfelder, Chardonnay, Bacchus, Pinot Gris

## TERROIR

Bolney Wine Estate is located on the edge of the South Downs, about 14 miles from the UK's South Coast, sitting at 25m (82 feet) above sea level. Comprising of five unique vineyard sites, it offers a combination of clay and sandstone - predominantly Upper Tunbridge Wells Sand, which allows good heat retention and excellent drainage. Chardonnay has been planted on a richer clay textured block, while the Bacchus sits in a particularly warm block to encourage higher ripeness levels.

The first grape variety to be planted in 1972 was Müller-Thurgau, a White grape varietal originating from Germany. Over the last 40 years, Bolney has grown 9 different varieties of Red and White grapes on their Estate, comprising of; Würzer, Pinot Gris, Müller-Thurgau, Bacchus, Chardonnay, Reichensteiner, Pinot Noir, Rondo and Dornfelder. Presently, it is focusing on 6 key premium varietals: Pinot Noir, Rondo, Dornfelder, Chardonnay, Bacchus and Pinot Gris. The vineyard team work tirelessly to provide extensive canopy management throughout the season to ensure the ideal microclimate, which in turn leads to a high quality fruit to produce award-winning still and sparkling wines.

## ABOUT

Bolney Wine Estate, a pioneer of English Wine, is one of England's oldest and most beautiful vineyards. A three-generation family business led by Sam Linter, they have been innovators of English wine since 1972 when their first vines were planted.

Bolney spent years innovating with experimental vines to identify the best varieties of grapes to grow in their eco-system. The South facing vineyards, paired with the mild climate and the sandstone soil, offer ideal conditions for English wine production. Guided by nature – Bolney believe that the more they understand and take inspiration from the nature around them, the more that they can appreciate its needs and protect its diversity and beauty for future generations. Sam, along with her expert team, combine their knowledge and expertise to create award-winning still and sparkling wines, as well as producing Rosso Vermouth and Bolney Estate Gin using foraged hedgerow fruits and herbs.

## THE WINE

Bolney has made its reputation on producing a variety of wine styles, encompassing Champagne varieties, as well as German varieties, both Red and White, which form part of the heritage of English wine.

Their still wines champion the now-typical English staples of Pinot Noir, Chardonnay, Bacchus and Pinot Gris, while their sparkling range encompasses both upfront, fruit-forward styles and more premium, lees-influenced blends.

Their goal is to produce wines which are approachable and fruit-driven, while respecting the distinctive English characteristics of bright acidity, food-friendliness and balance.

The focus in the winery is the preservation and enhancement of the fruity and floral characteristics inherent in the grape crop, with the influence of oxygen and oak carefully controlled.

### Cuvée Rosé

An elegant and delicate, single vintage, traditional method sparkling wine. A salmon pink colour in the glass full of lots of tiny bubbles. Floral and Red apple aromas lead to Red apple and cranberry on the palate with a bright, fresh finish and lovely length.

### Bolney Bubbly

Delightful floral and brioche notes combine with zesty citrus fruit, honeysuckle and elderflower. It is delicate and well balanced, finishing with a soft fresh hint of sweetness.

### Blanc de Blancs

A very stylish, single vintage, traditional method, quality Sussex sparkling wine. Elegant fruit and hazelnut aromas complement the smooth texture and creamy finish. Gentle fruit and lovely length.

### Eighteen Acre Rosé

A superb non-vintage, traditional method sparkling wine, with vibrant pink colour in the glass. Aromas of brioche and summer fruits, lead to raspberry ripple, Red apple and hints of pastry on the palate with a smooth, creamy finish.

### Cuvée Noir

A unique Red sparkling wine made using the

traditional method. Aromas reminiscent of Red stone fruits, especially Red cherry, redcurrants and sweet blueberries. On the palate, a wonderful creamy richness and full bodied mousse, packed full of ripe summer fruits, with a hint of sweet spice on the finish.

## Classic Cuvée

This is a fine sparkling wine made from the classic Champagne varieties: 60% Pinot Noir, 25% Pinot Meunier, 15% Chardonnay. Delightful hedgerow fruits and brioche notes combine with sweet apple and stone fruits. Fresh and elegant with a good body and persistent mousse.

## VISITING AND BUYING

Join Bolney at their welcoming, family-run estate, for one of their unique vineyard tours exploring their state-of-the-art winery – fascinating even for non-wine drinkers – before visiting the tasting room where all the fun of sampling happens. Why not take a stroll around the Vineyard Trail, which is designed for all the family to enjoy, before taking a seat in the Eighteen Acre Café that has a stunning viewing balcony overlooking the ripening vines? It's a great place for a spot of lunch with guests or with the family (including dogs) or simply catching up with friends. All food is locally sourced, offering their chef's freshest seasonal ingredients to create delicious dishes for breakfast and lunch – the perfect accompaniment to their award-wining wines.

Open daily, year-round. For tours and tastings, events or to discover their award-winning range visit:
www.bolneywineestate.com
Telephone: 01444 881575
Press enquiries: media@bolneywineestate.com
Email: info@bolneywineestate.com

# BREAKY BOTTOM VINEYARD

## EAST SUSSEX

BREAKY BOTTOM, RODMELL, LEWES, EAST SUSSEX BN7 3EX

- 2.2 Ha of planted vines

- 10,000–12,000 bottles annually

- Winemaker Peter Hall

- Grape varieties Seyval Blanc, Chardonnay, Pinot Noir, Pinot Meunier

### TERROIR

Breaky Bottom is set in an isolated valley in the South Downs National Park. Peter also cares for a small flock of around 25 ewes and lambs to graze the surrounding steep banks. The soil is a free-draining chalk loam with flint. They are just two miles from the English Channel, a secluded valley offering shelter from coastal winds and providing an ideal microclimate for vine growing. Proximity to the sea also minimises the risk of spring frost. This is a small-scale family-run business producing top quality wines that command a premium in the market. In a typical year this might amount to 12,000 bottles, although in some years the entire crop has been lost to floods or pheasants! They risk harvesting as late as possible in the autumn to maximise ripeness and allow the full expression of Breaky Bottom's unique terroir.

## ABOUT

Peter has always produced wine from grapes grown only in this valley. He originally planted the vineyard back in 1974 with Seyval Blanc and Muller-Thurgau, and established Breaky Bottom's reputation making still dry White wines. The 1990 vintage Seyval Blanc won a Gold Medal in the 1993 International Wine Challenge. For years they felt the Seyval Blanc would make great fizz. It had such a clean fresh taste and retained good acidity even when fully ripe. They produced their first sparkling brut made with 100% Seyval Blanc in 1995, released in 2000 as 'Millennium Cuvée Maman Mercier', dedicated to Peter's mother. Peter has since focused purely on sparkling wines, adding the three Champagne varieties in 2002 and 2004.

Following their first sparkling vintage they have dedicated each cuvée to honour friends and family that have been important in their life. Reynolds Stone, for example, the famous wood engraver and designer of the original Breaky Bottom label is celebrated in the 2010 Chardonnay/Pinot. Nobel Prize winner Sir Harry Kroto and cartoonist Gerard Hoffnung are just two of Peter's friends commemorated in this way.

## THE WINE

They make two cuvées each year, a Seyval Blanc and a Chardonnay/Pinot blend, and age them in bottle for at least four years. Compared to most wineries, production is very modest. About 6,000 bottles of each cuvée are made and are all individually numbered. Nine wines are currently available. The oldest vintages, 2009/10/11, are now only available under 'Limited Allocation'.

**2009 Chardonnay, Pinot Noir, Pinot Meunier**
Limited Allocation
Cuvée Gerard Hoffnung

**2010 Seyval Blanc**
Limited Allocation. Cuvée Koizumi Yakumo

**2010 Chardonnay, Pinot Noir, Pinot Meunier**
Limited Allocation. Cuvée Reynolds Stone

**2011 Chardonnay, Seyval Blanc, Pinot Noir and Pinot Meunier**
Cuvée Oliver Minkley.

**2013 Chardonnay, Seyval Blanc, Pinot Noir and Pinot Meunier**
Cuvée Cornelis Hendriksen.

**2014 Seyval Blanc**
Cuvée Peter Christiansen.

**2014 Chardonnay, Pinot Noir and Pinot Meunier**
Cuvée Michelle Moreau.

**2015 Seyval Blanc**
Cuvée Jack Pike.

**2015 Chardonnay, Pinot Noir and Pinot Meunier**
Cuvée David Pearson.

## VISITING AND BUYING

Breaky Bottom is not just a vineyard, it is also their home. They are pleased to welcome visitors, but by appointment only. A full tour and tasting, usually for a minimum of six people, costs £15 a head.
www.breakybottom.co.uk

# CARR TAYLOR

## EAST SUSSEX

YEW TREE FARM, WHEEL LANE, WESTFIELD, TN35 4SG

- 14.5 Ha **of planted vines**
- 30,000 **bottles annually**
- **Winemaker Alex Carr Taylor**
- **Vintage information Carr Taylor Brut 2015, Rosé Sparkling 2015, Bacchus 2020**
- **Grape varieties Reichensteiner, Bacchus, Ortega, Pinot Noir, Pinot Meunier, Dornfelder, Pinot Blanc, Wurzer, Schonburger, Chardonnay, Gutenborner**

## TERROIR

The vineyard is situated on the edge of the Sussex weald in an Area of Outstanding National Beauty in the south east corner of the UK. The climate is generally warm and dry and benefits from the warmth of its location being 8 km (5 miles) from the coast.

The vines are planted on gently undulating fields on a free draining sandy loam over sandstone bedrock. The whole site is sheltered by hedgerows and old chestnut coppices which enhances the local climate. Minimal tilling and the growth of wild flowers adds to the health of the soils.

## ABOUT

David and Linda Carr Taylor realised their ambition of planting a vineyard when, in 1969, David purchased 21 acres of land surrounding his family home in the beautiful East Sussex countryside.

The initial planting commenced in 1971 with varieties such as Reichensteiner, Gutenborner, Muller Thurgau, Dornfelder and the classic Champagne varieties.

The glorious summer of 1976 heralded the first commercially viable harvest for the vineyard and some 2000 bottles of Carr Taylor wines were produced! Since then, Carr Taylor has gone from strength to strength winning their first award in 1983 in the International Wine & Spirit Competition. The following years have seen a succession of medals in international competitions, accruing in excess of 150 awards.

In 1983 an exceptional harvest encouraged the vineyard to experiment with sparkling wine. This venture produced 10,000 bottles of traditionally fermented sparkling wine and resulted in the first commercially available Champagne Method English Sparkling Wine.

## THE WINE

### Carr Taylor Brut

Pale golden with subtle aromas of fresh apple and elderflower, their Brut Sparkling Wine is racy and fresh. Bottle maturation provides hints of biscuit on the nose, and butter on the palate. Using different grape varieties to Champagne results in slightly less austere, more aromatic, fruity flavours which have proved to be consistently popular over the years.

### Carr Taylor Demi Sec

This wine has a gentle golden colour and a soft peachy nose with hints of apple and vanilla. The fresh fruit flavours have a subtle complexity and a luscious, sweet finish.

A rich velvety mouth feel and a creamy mousse crown this superior sparkling wine.

### Carr Taylor Rosé Sparkling

The Pinot Noir and Dornfelder grapes lend a delicate pink shade to the wine and a fresh raspberry and redcurrant streak on the palate. The soft acidity and hint of sweetness give this wine the perfect character for celebrating with friends.

### Carr Taylor White Pinot

An equal blend of fresh, crisp Pinot Blanc and the subtle fruit of Pinot Noir; an outstanding example of the elegance that can be achieved in England's cool climate. The perfumed nose of White peach and brioche is followed by an invigorating palate of taut minerality that compliments the White fruit and apricot notes. With hints of toast from bottle age which lends creaminess and a fine silky mousse, the complexity of flavours persist in the long, clean finish.

### Carr Taylor Rosé

Mid cherry pink in colour, this wine has a delightfully subtle nose of raspberries and cherries. Typical English crispness complements the soft Red fruit flavours. Ideal with barbecues, pork or poultry roasts, smoked foods or rich White meat. A taste of summer in a glass!

## VISITING AND BUYING

Open 10am–5pm Daily
General Enquiries 01424 752501
Email: sales@carr-taylor.co.uk
www.carr-taylor.co.uk

# Spotlight on
# CHAPEL DOWN

## KENT

THE CHAPEL DOWN WINERY, SMALL HYTHE, TENTERDEN, KENT, TN30 7NG

CHAPEL DOWN
TENTERDEN ENGLAND

- 316 Ha **of planted vines**
- 1 million **bottles of traditional method sparkling wine annually**
- Winemakers **Josh Donaghay-Spire (Winemaker) Jo Arkle (Assistant Winemaker)**
- Grape varieties **Chardonnay, Pinot Noir, Pinot Blanc, Pinot Meunier**

## TERROIR

Chapel Down now sources fruit from 316 Ha (780 acres) of land across the South-East of England for it's sparkling and still wines. The majority of this land is on the Kent North Downs, with some exceptional sites at Kit's Coty Vineyard, Boxley and Boarley. The free-draining chalk soils provide the perfect terroir for producing well balanced, intensely flavoured fruit. Restricting yields and maintaining vine balance allow vines to fulfil their potential, producing fruit that truly express their identity and the unique qualities of the soil. At harvest time fruit is picked by hand and transported to their Winery just outside Tenterden, Kent.

## ABOUT

Chapel Down is England's leading winemaker with a desire to change the way the world thinks about English wine forever by making the coolest, cool climate wines on the planet accessible and contemporary. Truly world-class sparkling and still wines are produced from grapes grown in the excellent terroir in the South East of England.

Chapel Down pushes the boundaries of wine production in England and continually strives to innovate in all areas of the business and create exceptional wines with a freshness of character.

Regularly receiving international accolades Chapel Down is also an official wine supplier to 10 Downing Street and is the first English winery to ever feature in the London Stock Exchange's 1,000 Companies to Inspire Britain. Their multi award-winning drinks are sold direct to consumers

through a fast growing e-commerce business and to retail partners, including Waitrose, M&S, Sainsbury's, Tesco, Majestic, Selfridges and Harrods, as well as leading bars, restaurants and hotels in the UK and internationally.

The Chapel Down Winery is open to the public and welcomes over 60,000 visitors each year.

## THE WINE

### Kit's Coty Coeur de Cuvée 2015
Produced from the very best blocks of Chardonnay within the Kit's Coty estate. The Coeur de Cuvée 2015 is made from the 'heart of the first pressing', the finest quality portion of juice extracted exclusively from the first press cycle.

A rich, elegant English Sparkling Wine with aromas of melon, peach and hints of butter and toast. The palate has incredible purity and finesse,

coming from a combination of the chalk soils and the specific pressing technique which carries the well-integrated oak and fruit characters perfectly. IWC 2021 Silver Medal Winner

## Chapel Down Rosé Brut

A delightful traditional method sparkling wine made from 100% Pinot Noir grapes from Kent, Sussex and Essex. Cool fermentation in stainless steel followed by partial malolactic fermentation. Maturation on fine lees in tank for six months before bottling and an average of 18 months further ageing on lees in bottle. A delicate Rosé with fruity notes which makes a perfect aperitif.

## Chapel Down Brut NV

Their flagship sparkling wine is widely available in major retailers as well as hospitality venues and makes a fantastic introduction to quality English Sparkling Wine. Chapel Down Brut NV is an elegant blend of four classic grape varieties and spends 18 months on its lees before release. Aromas of Red apple, citrus fruits and freshly baked bread together with hints of strawberry and quince and fine, persistent bubbles.

## VISITING AND BUYING

The Chapel Down Winery is open to visitors throughout the year for tours, tastings and experiences.
**Visit www.chapeldown.com or call 01580 766111 for more details.**

# CHARLES PALMER VINEYARDS

## EAST SUSSEX

CHARLES PALMER VINEYARDS, WICKHAM MANOR, WICKHAM ROCK LANE, WINCHELSEA, EAST SUSSEX, ENGLAND, TN36 4AG

- **14 Ha** of planted vines

- **50,000** bottles annually

- **Winemakers Will Davenport (up to 2017 followed by consultant wine maker) Charles Palmer and son, Robert Palmer**

- **Vintage information 2018 was the most amazing year so far in their history, the** weather was ideal from start to finish with perfect growing and ripening conditions. It was so good that they were able to leave picking of one of their Pinot Noir blocks for one week after they had finished the main picking and then make their first still Red wine.

- **Grape varieties Chardonnay and Pinot Noir**

## TERROIR

The estate's vineyards benefit from an ideal climate for vines, with its close proximity to the sea, south facing slope, and its terroir in particular. The lowest part of the vineyard is a mere 5 metres (16.4 feet) from sea level and sits above a bed of Kimmeridgian clay similar to the Grand Crus of Burgundy.

## ABOUT

Charles Palmer Vineyards is a family run wine estate at Winchelsea in Sussex.

Their vines were first planted in 2006 specifically with the aim of producing a sparkling wine of the highest standard. Production is small and meticulous. Every effort is made to ensure only the best grapes are produced and selected according to the family's exacting standards. The result is a small and exciting collection of vintage sparkling wines, each vintage unique and characterful in its own way.

## THE WINE

### Blanc de Blancs 2014

Apricot, peach and citrus notes blended with brioche aromas. This is a great vintage to get stuck into early. Made with 100% of their Chardonnay grapes, it spends 3 years on lees. Platinum winner at The Decanter World Wine Awards 2019.

### Classic Cuvée 2014

Flavours of honey, tropical fruits, vanilla and almonds with a hint of peach and fig. This wine is a 60/40 blend of their Pinot Noir and Chardonnay grapes. It has spent 3 years on the lees.

### Rosé 2016

Their Rosé is made from one particular parcel of their Pinot Noir grapes. The grapes are low yielding Burgundy clones that are of exceptional quality and it spends 3 years on the lees.

## VISITING AND BUYING

Open by appointment
Telephone: 01797 226216
Email:
vineyard@charlespalmer-vineyards.co.uk
www.charlespalmer-vineyards.co.uk

# COURT GARDEN

## EAST SUSSEX

COURT GARDENS FARM, ORCHARD LANE, DITCHLING, EAST SUSSEX, BN6 8TH

- 7 Ha **of planted vines**

- 30,000-40,000 **bottles annually**

- **Winemaker Hugo Corney**

- **Vintage Information Blanc de Blancs 2015 / Ditchling White 2018**

- **Grape varieties Chardonnay, Pinot Noir, Pinot Meunier, Pinot Gris, Pinot Blanc, Pinot Noir Précose, Rondo. Two old Champagne varieties Arbanne and Petit Meslier are also grown**

## TERROIR

A beautiful south-facing slope with the South Downs as a backdrop. In the foot of the South Downs the vineyard sits on a mix of green sand and Sussex clay. The vineyard's maritime climate, while protected in the lea of the downs, originates from the south westerly Atlantic airstream.

## ABOUT

Court Garden is a family-run, single-estate vineyard and winery within the South Downs National Park. Court Garden is a working sheep farm which diversified into viticulture in 2005.

While the farm still has sheep the principle activities relate to the vineyard and winery.

## THE WINE

Court Garden is passionate about the grapes that they grow and the wine that they make. In recent years, that passion has been rewarded with numerous national and international awards; most notably two prestigious International Wine Challenge trophies, plus gold medals in 50 Great Sparkling Wines of the World, the International Wine Challenge, the International Wine & Spirit Competition, UK Vineyards Association and Sommelier Wine Awards.

They produce a range of five sparkling wines and three still wines and the Blanc de Blancs is the flagship cuvée.

### Court Garden Classic Cuvée 2015 Vintage
Decanter World Wine Awards 2020 Silver Decanter World Wine Awards 2019 Silver IWSC 2019 Silver IWSC 2020 Bronze IWC 2019 Bronze

Current Awards: Decanter World Wine Awards 2020 Silver, Decanter World Wine Awards 2019 Silver, IWSC 2019 Silver, IWSC 2020 Bronze, IWC 2019 Bronze.

Pale silver lime-leaf green, continuous small bubbles; toasty, under-ripe pineapple and greengage fruit behind; Brut-style, balanced with creamy mousse and great freshness, long finish.

### Court Garden Rosé 2015 Vintage
Very pale peach hue, frothy; dried cranberry, autolytic; nicely defined Red fruit flavours, lively acidity balancing creamy mousse and good weight, nicely balanced, savoury finish with a lovely brioche character. Lovely on its own or with perhaps a few canapés, some charcuterie or smoked fish.

### Court Garden Blanc de Noirs 2013 Vintage
IWC 2018 Bronze
Current Awards: IWC 2018 Bronze

Silver lime-leaf green, fine fizz; good yeast autolysis and green fruit with lemon grass accent; lovely delicate style with good balance between acidity and dosage. Nicely defined mid-palate with rich flavour, clean and crisp finish.

### Court Garden Blanc de Blancs 2015 Vintage
IWC 2020 Silver IWSC 2020 Silver Decanter World Wine Awards 2020 Silver

Current Awards: IWSC 2020 Silver, Decanter World Wine Awards 2020 Silver

The International Wine Challenge judges described their 2011 Blanc de Blancs as 'Gentle and elegant style. Sliced green apples and Gala melon. Fine boned with persistent chalky length'.

### Court Garden Ditchling Quartet 2014 Vintage
A delicious Pinot Noir / Pinot Précose dominant wine blended with small amounts of Pinot Meunier and Chardonnay from the wonderful 2014 vintage. 60% of the wine spent six months in French oak barrel, to add richness and softness to the mouthfeel. Great finesse and complexity coupled with Red berry fruits and hints of vanilla on the finish.

## VISITING AND BUYING

Open to visitors by appointment, mostly Friday / Saturday.
Website: www.courtgarden.com
Telephone: 01273 844479
Email: wine@courtgarden.com

# DAVENPORT VINEYARDS

## KENT AND EAST SUSSEX

LIMNEY FARM, CASTLE HILL, ROTHERFIELD, EAST SUSSEX TN6 3RR
HAZEL STREET FARM, HORSMONDEN, KENT TN12 8EF

- 9 Ha **of planted vines**

- 30,000 to 50,000 **bottles annually (around 15,000 to 20,000 bottles of sparkling wine)**

- **Winemaker Will Davenport**

- **Vintage information current vintage sold is 2015**

- **Grape varieties Chardonnay, Pinot Noir, Pinot Meunier**

## TERROIR

Chardonnay and Pinot Meunier grapes are grown in Kent on a sandy soil in a very sheltered position, planted in 2007, and are organic certified.

The Pinot Noir comes from their East Sussex vineyard on a West facing slope with loam and sandstone soils, more exposed to the wind which keeps temperatures down and helps to prevent mildew. Organic certified.

## ABOUT

Davenport Vineyards started in 1991 with a focus on making still White wines. The first sparkling wines were made in 1997 and in 2000 all the vineyards were converted to organic management. Nearly 30 years after the first vines were planted still wines make up 60% of annual production, but sparkling wine production is increasing. The 2008 Limney Estate sparkling wine was awarded the Gore-Browne trophy for the best UK wine of that year and many vintages have been awarded Gold medals in several UK and international competitions.

Will Davenport has made huge efforts to reduce the environmental impact of the wine production process over the last 10 years. The winery is self-sufficient for electricity and all packaging is minimal (and all recyclable). The land around the vineyard is managed to maximise biodiversity.

## THE WINE

The 2015 Limney Estate sparkling wine is made from organic grapes using the traditional bottle-fermented method. 10% of the blend is fermented in large oak barrels and no yeast is added to the wines for the primary fermentation. Wines are blended and bottled without any fining or filtration. After bottling, the wine is matured on the yeast sediment for 5 years before disgorging. The emphasis is on making wine that is allowed to express the character of the grapes, without being manipulated by the winemaker.

### Limney Estate 2015

The 2015 newly released, is made from 80% Chardonnay, 12% Pinot Noir and 8% Pinot Meunier. With 5 years maturing in the bottle on lees, it has plenty of yeast character combined with the surprisingly youthful fruit. This is a wine that is delicious now and will develop further over the long term.

### Limney Estate Sparkling Rosé 2016

New in 2014, this is their third vintage as sparkling Rosé, made from 70% Chardonnay and 30% Pinot Noir. The wine has a light rose colour and shows the characters of Pinot Noir, with the backbone of the Chardonnay giving it some structure.

### 2013 Blanc de Blancs sparkling wine

This is a one-off wine, 100% organic Chardonnay, made in a completely natural way, without yeast added (primary fermentation), unfiltered and with no added sulphur. It was fermented in a single oak barrique (225 litres barrel) with the intention of blending it into the Limney Estate sparkling wine of the same vintage to add a touch of complexity, but when they tasted it there was no question of blending such a good wine. It was bottled straight from the barrel and matured on yeast lees in the bottle for 5 years before disgorging. The wine has a rich mature style, amazing length of flavour and complexity – this is a fascinating wine for those who love rare and unusual sparkling wines. A complete treat. Only 275 bottles were made.

## VISITING AND BUYING

Davenport Vineyards is not open to the public, but wines can be purchased on their website or from a range of independent wine shops around the UK.
www.davenportvineyards.co.uk
Email: info@davenportvineyards.co.uk
Telephone: 01892 852380

*Spotlight on*
# DENBIES WINE ESTATE

## SURREY

DORKING, SURREY, RH5 6AA

- **87 Ha** of planted vines
- **450,000** bottles annually
- **Winemakers** John Worontschak and Matthieu Elzinga
- **Grape varieties** Chardonnay, Pinot Noir, Pinot Meunier, Bacchus

## TERROIR

The unique characteristics of the North Downs landscape with its south facing slopes, chalky soil and micro-climate, make it ideal for creating one of England's largest vineyards. Denbies Wine Estate produces internationally award-winning, cool climate sparkling wines using the traditional grape varieties, grown on chalky soil. It has also an excellent reputation for producing world-class premium still wines.

## ABOUT

Denbies Wine Estate, one of England's largest vineyards, is situated on the outskirts of Dorking in the Surrey Hills. Approaching the expansive Denbies Estate, for a moment, one could really be anywhere in the world, acres and acres of vineyard rolling into the distant hills, a captivating sight in the middle of Surrey. On-site facilities include tours, tastings, an art gallery, shopping, a brewery, a local farm shop, restaurants, a Vineyard Hotel, Surrey Hills Health & Wellbeing Centre and Paradox Parlour Escape Rooms. Denbies is an all-weather destination in the heart of Surrey Hills wine country.

## THE WINE

### Denbies Whitedowns NV

This wine offers fresh citrus aromas with just a hint of brioche. The palate is crisp, dry and refreshing thanks to its finely balanced acidity. It has an enticing creamy texture and a persistent length of flavour. 12.5% vol 75cl and 9.2 g/l Residual Sugar.

### Denbies Greenfields NV

Medium golden straw in colour Greenfields displays an elegant and sustained mousse. The nose shows some developed, yeasty complexity with brioche and strawberry notes combined with hints of vanilla and lavender. Made from 85% Pinot Noir, 13.5% Chardonnay and 1.5% Pinot Meunier the palate is creamy, layered and structured with a crisp finish and great length.

### Denbies Sparkling Bacchus NV

Pale straw green in colour with an elegant and persistent mousse the Denbies Sparkling Bacchus is bursting with fresh honeysuckle, Red fruits and rose petal on the nose. The palate is lean and crisp with a zingy citrus fruit acidity culminating in a long and creamy finish. Perfect on its own as an aperitif or with air dried ham, mild cheeses or even with White asparagus. 100% Bacchus

## VISITING AND BUYING

Visitors to the estate have the opportunity to sample the range of 16 wines. Indoor winery and outdoor vineyard train tours take place daily which can be booked online. The winery centre also hosts a Wine and Gift Shop, Art Gallery and local Village Greens Farm Shop. Wine purchases can be made in person in their Wine and Gift Shop or online at **www.denbies.co.uk**

# *Spotlight on*
# DIGBY FINE ENGLISH

## SUSSEX

DIGBY FINE ENGLISH, 55-57 HIGH STREET, ARUNDEL, BN18 9AJ

## TERROIR

After a lot of tasting and travelling across the South East, Digby have identified and built relationships with the top 1% of English vineyards. To make the cut, a vineyard has to be a proven, already-in-production site, with a keen pursuit for sustainability and representing a distinct facet of English terroir. Digby are very proud of their portfolio of growers, so much so that they are top secret! Individual quality and collective variety = blended magic. This process has made Digby

- 120,000 **bottles annually**

- CEO and Head Blender **Trevor Clough**

- Vintage information **2010 Blanc de Noirs, 2013 Vintage Reserve Brut, 2014 Vintage Rosé**

- Grape varieties **Pinot Noir, Chardonnay and Pinot Meunier**

unique in England, as they are the first négociant or blending house in this country.

## ABOUT

Digby Fine English is a négociant rather than a vineyard – a first for the UK. Working with specially selected growers in Dorset, Kent, Sussex and Hampshire.

Digby Fine English launched its first wines for sale in 2013 in Selfridges, won its first trophy in 2014 and has gone on to great adventures around the world in the years since then. It is a bold and exuberant modern brand of luxury English Sparkling Wine. Digby Fine English can be found in Selfridges, Harvey Nichols, Fortnum & Mason and Waitrose.

## THE WINE

Over the last five to ten years the industry has seen a very new trend: sparkling wine made with the traditional method and traditional varieties of Pinot Noir, Chardonnay and Pinot Meunier, proven round the world to produce a wine with a high degree of finesse. This trend is coupled with the ideal growing conditions for these varieties in South East England to produce flavourful grapes for sparkling wine: comprised of the chalky soil that starts with the White Cliffs of Dover and the weather with a long, cool growing season.

### 2013 Vintage Reserve Brut

Elegant yet bold, Digby's internationally renowned flagship sparkling wine is a blend of Chardonnay, Pinot Noir and Pinot Meunier grapes hand-harvested in English wine country in October 2013. Digby's flagship style is considered to be one of the best expressions of what is unique and world-class about English sparkling terroir, having won the 2019 World Championships Trophy as the top vintage wine produced in their Nation.

### 2010 Blanc de Noirs Brut

The first Digby wine to earn their Long-Aged moniker launched June 2020, initially only available to Kenelm Club Members. This is Digby's first ever Blanc de Noirs which showcases the best Pinot Red grapes from a decade ago. A white fizz made only

with red grapes, it is a beautiful expression of what is unique about English wine, and deftly shows the magic of traditional method sparkling winemaking. With only 1,500 bottles created, this is the latest gem in the Digby crown.

### 2014 Vintage Rosé

With a resounding generosity, this 2014 Vintage Rosé is inspired by Digby's best Pinot Noir fruit since 2009. Creamy elegance gives way to a gentlemanly richness: imagine Sir Kenelm Digby savouring a glass while reading a book in his famed library. Years of ageing accentuates the power of this fizz, making Digby's Rosé a highly versatile companion to food.

### Leander Pink NV Brut

This pink fizz is a blend that celebrates England's most vibrant Pinot Noir fruit, with Red berry aromas carried on the back of a light, creamy fruitiness. Every bottle sold supports Leander Academy, training new talent to become the world champions of the future.

### Non Vintage Brut

Vibrant yet understated, this fizz is in its element at home on a Tuesday evening or at a party celebrating one of life's big moments. An engaging expression of Digby's house style, it stems from England's most luscious Pinot Noir with rich, aged Chardonnay and plummy Pinot Meunier.

## VISITING AND BUYING

www.digby-fine-english.com
Telephone: 020 7112 8887
Email: cheers@digbyfineenglish.com
Tasting Rooms 55-57 High St, Arundel, BN18, 9AJ, UK.

# ELHAM VALLEY VINEYARD

## KENT

ELHAM VALLEY VINEYARD, BREACH, BARHAM, KENT, CT4 6LN

- 1 Ha of planted vines
- 1,000 bottles annually
- Winemaker Defined Wines
- Vintage information 2015, 2016, 2019
- Grape varieties Pinot Noir and Seyval Blanc

## TERROIR

The Elham Valley is a designated Kent Downs Area of Outstanding Natural Beauty (AONB) between Canterbury and Folkestone, and here you will find the eponymous vineyard belonging to The Fifth Trust, a charity supporting adults with learning disabilities.

Elham Valley Vineyard is one of the longest established in East Kent, originally cultivated in 1985, and replanted in 2011 with Bacchus (no longer harvested), Pinot Noir and Seyval varieties.

## ABOUT

The Fifth Trust's horticultural students, who are among 150 learning disabled adults who attend a day centre at the vineyard offering a wide range of educational and creative sessions, play an active role in tending the vines and harvesting the grapes. With the opening of winemaker Defined Wines in Bridge, the wine's journey from vine to bottle is now less than eight km (five miles).

The site is also home to The Fifth Trust's Vineyard garden centre and café, with a terrace overlooking the vines, where visitors can enjoy a glass of Elham Valley Vineyard sparkling and still wines and purchase bottles to take home.

Informal tours of the vineyard, as well as the skills centre where students create pottery and woodwork for sale, are available on request.

## THE WINE

### 2016 Sparkling Rosé

A really fresh attractive nose with gentle raspberry notes and hints of brioche. Created from Pinot Noir grapes, the wine delivers a mouthful of bright fruits with fine mousse and a silky finish. A lovely wine for a summer's day.

### 2016 Sparkling

A sparkling Seyval with a fresh nose of apple and brioche and a crisp, dry palate offering a gentle mousse and flavours of fresh bread, lemon and yellow apple. The finish is long and delightfully mealy.

### 2019 White

This clean and bright Seyval blend displays pretty White stone fruit and green apple on the nose followed by White peach and grapefruit on the palette. The wine is well balanced with the acidity complemented by the nettle and elderflower notes, which give way to a soft yet lengthy finish.

## VISITING AND BUYING

The Vineyard Garden Centre and Café are open seven days a week. Monday–Saturday 9am-4pm; Sunday 10am–4pm. Informal tours conducted whenever staff are available, or organised group events with wine tasting can be booked.

Wine sales from the licensed café and garden centre.

www.vineyardgardencentre.co.uk
www.fifthtrust.co.uk
Telephone: 01227 832022
Email: info@fifthtrust.co.uk

# GREYFRIARS VINEYARD

## SURREY

### THE HOG'S BACK, PUTTENHAM, GUILDFORD GU3 1AG

- 16.2 Ha of planted vines

- Average 80,000–100,000 bottles annual production

- Winemaker Mike Wagstaff

- Grape varieties Chardonnay, Pinot Noir, Pinot Meunier, Sauvignon Blanc, Pinot Gris, Pinot Blanc

## TERROIR

Greyfriars is located on the sunny south facing chalk slopes of the Hog's Back (A31) at Puttenham, just outside Guildford and Farnham in Surrey. They produce a range of spectacular English wines reflecting the unique local soil conditions, climate and heritage of the Surrey North Downs. The geology is the same free-draining chalk as occurs in Champagne and is great for Pinot Noir and Chardonnay in particular.

## ABOUT

In 2010, husband and wife Mike and Hilary Wagstaff made their vinous dreams come true when they took over Greyfriars Vineyard. The original vineyard plot was planted in 1989 with Chardonnay and Pinot Noir, one of the first vineyards in England to plant these traditional Champagne grape varieties.

David Line, former rock star-turned-vineyard-manager and brother-in-law, swiftly came on board after Mike and Hilary took over and together they have expanded the area under vine to 16.2 Ha (40 acres) across two sites focusing on producing stunning English Sparkling Wine. In addition to a state-of-the-art winemaking facility, the team dug into the side of the chalky hills behind their winery to develop a 3,500 square foot natural chalk underground cellar for ageing their wine prior to release. The cave is the perfect underground storage facility with a capacity of 250,000 bottles and natural temperature control – it is a truly beautiful site to behold.

The Wagstaffs' impressive level of vision and investment hasn't stopped there – in 2021 Greyfriars opened a brand new 100-person capacity Tasting Room, a beautifully constructed modern events space that has added to the charming estate. In addition to vineyard tours and tastings, the vineyard now also runs a wine bar, music events, events with local artisan producers and even yoga in the vines.

The vineyard focuses on producing high quality sparkling and still wines with a grape to glass approach. Their wines have won many prizes in international competitions, including a Gold Outstanding in the 2018 International Wine & Spirit Competition and the coveted English Sparkling Rosé Trophy in the 2019 International Wine Challenge. More recently, their 2015 Rosé Reserve won a Gold Medal with 95 points in the 2021 International Wine Challenge. This plucky young producer from the Surrey Hills has stacked up nicely against the very best wines in the world and we cannot wait to see what Mike, Hilary, David and the team will do next.

## THE WINE

The Greyfriars range currently contains 15 different wines. Here are some highlights:

### 2017 Rosé Reserve

This is now the sixth release of their 'signature' IWC Gold Medal award winning wine. The 2016 vintage at Greyfriars was fairly challenging with a cold wet start to the ripening season, however, a late Indian Summer came to their rescue and the grapes were lovingly handpicked in the middle of October. This wine is made from the best Pinot Noir grapes from their Monkshatch vineyard, to produce a fresh and fruity rosé, full of flavours of summer berries.

### "X" – 2017 Blanc de Noirs

2021 marks 10 years since Mike and Hilary took over Greyfriars and this wine has been specially created to celebrate that anniversary. This amazing wine has been produced using 100% Pinot Noir from the under-rated 2017 vintage and is a fantastic expression of their Pinot Noir grapes which seem to be at the heart of their most exciting wines.

### 2014 Unoaked Blanc de Blancs

A pure Chardonnay wine is vibrant and crisp with delicious lemony and other citrus notes. A true English classic.

### Non Vintage Cuvée

This non-vintage blend of reserve wines from 2014, 2015 and 2016, which they keep in tanks to maintain a consistency in style and develop a complexity in flavour over time. Fresh and fruity, the wine is soft and dry with intense lemon, apple and mineral flavours.

### 2014 Classic Cuvée

An elegant and complex wine, with layers of citrusy fruits and a vibrant mineral finish. The tension and ripe citrus fruits of this dry sparkling wine works particularly well with Thai-inspired recipes. The roundness and subtle mouthfeel of the wine is a treat to match with noble fish and seafood.

## VISITING AND BUYING

Buy online at www.greyfriarsvineyard.co.uk with nationwide home/office delivery.
Telephone: 01483 818712
Email: info@greyfriarsvineyard.co.uk
Visit www.greyfriarsvineyard.co.uk for more information.

# GUSBOURNE ESTATE

## KENT & WEST SUSSEX

GUSBOURNE ESTATE, KENARDINGTON ROAD, APPLEDORE, ASHFORD, KENT TN26 2BE

GUSBOURNE

- **90 Ha of planted vines (60 in Kent and 30 in West Sussex)**

- Winemaker
  **Charlie Holland**

- Vintage information
  **Blanc de Blancs 2016**

- Grape variety
  **Chardonnay**

## TERROIR

In Kent the soils are a mix of clay and sandy loam. They also find some marine deposits in the soil profile as their land was once swamp and marsh land. They are just ten km (six miles) from the coast on low lying soil and enjoy good levels of sunshine and warm breezes in summer. The resulting wine style from these vineyards is relatively round and generous.

The majority of their vineyards are in Kent, with 60 hectares (148 acres) of plantings, so this forms the backbone of their wines. They are fortunate to also have 30 hectares (74 acres) in Sussex, which is planted on chalk. The style they see here is different with more acidity and minerality in the wines. The Sussex fruit can act as the backbone of the wine, while Kent gives a broader style. They work very well in support of each other and it's great to be able to blend these components to look to achieve a wine with real balance and poise.

## ABOUT

At Gusbourne, they produce exclusively vintage wines. They have a clear vision and a single goal: to create English Sparkling Wines that stand up alongside the very finest offerings from across the globe.

They believe that the only way to ensure the quality of their grapes (Chardonnay, Pinot Noir and Pinot Meunier) is to grow them themselves. That's why they plant predominantly Burgundian clones and why all the grapes used in their winemaking are sourced solely from Gusbourne vineyards.

Their winemaking is a slow and measured process and they follow strict, self-imposed parameters to maintain their exacting quality standards.

In 2010, their debut vintages of Gusbourne Brut Reserve 2006 and Gusbourne Blanc de Blancs 2006 were released to critical acclaim and they quickly earned a reputation as a producer of outstanding quality wines, with accolades from some of the industry's most exacting critics. They are the proud recipients of over 235 medals at local, regional and international level where they are compared to the finest wines from around the world.

## THE WINE

### Gusbourne Brut Reserve

Brut Reserve is their most robust expression of who they are and what they believe in: creating wines that are an authentic reflection of a time and place. Bright gold in colour, this classic blend of Chardonnay, Pinot Noir and Pinot Meunier highlights Red fruit aromas of cherry and strawberry, which then develop into attractive fresh pastry notes. With a bridge of citrus fruit, the palate is clean and fresh while giving tonnes of soft stone fruit and a long, refreshing finish.

Their 2015 is bright golden in colour, with aromas of green apple, ripe pear and candied citrus. The palate is fruit driven, with zesty mandarin, peach and apple pie. Hints of ginger and mineral notes combine with toasted nuts and brioche, leading to a long, elegant finish.

### Gusbourne Blanc de Blancs

A wine that typifies the linear purity of classic Blanc de Blancs. They select the finest lots of Chardonnay, exhibiting natural minerality, ensuring that the wine has both the finesse and elegance that one would expect in this style, but also the requisite qualities for extended ageing. A bright golden colour with a delicate mousse, their Blanc de Blancs has classic Chardonnay aromas of green apple, citrus and mineral notes combined with buttered toast and Tarte Tatin richness from extended lees ageing.

Their 2016 vintage has enjoyed a minimum of 42 months on its lees and is bright golden in colour with aromas of preserved lemon, ripe pear and brioche. The palate is rich and elegant, with candied citrus, stone fruits and toasted hazelnuts. A complex wine with attractive mineral notes and a long, rounded finish.

### Gusbourne Rosé

Their Rosé is unique to each growing season, a direct reflection of English summer and the grapes used to craft it. Delicate pink in appearance, with soft summer berries and floral notes on the nose. The palate shows bright red fruits, driven by ripe strawberries, fresh cherries and redcurrants, with a crisp freshness and creamy, rounded texture on the finish. A perfect expression of halcyon days.

The 2015 vintage is delicate pink in appearance, aromas of cherry, wild strawberry and cranberry combine with more developed brioche and fresh pastry notes. The palate balances soft summer pudding fruits, a vibrant citrus streak and a long and rounded finish.

## VISITING AND BUYING

Open daily, 10am to 5pm, for tours and tastings.
01233 758666
Tours and Tastings: nest@gusbourne.com
Press enquiries: jonathan.white@ gusbourne.com

# HENNERS VINEYARD

## EAST SUSSEX

HENNERS, CHURCH ROAD, HERSTMONCEUX, EAST SUSSEX BN27 1RJ

- 3 Ha **of planted vines**
- 150,000 **bottles annually**
- **Winemaker Collette O'Leary**
- **Vintage information 2014**
- **Grape varieties Pinot Noir and Chardonnay, Pinot Munier**

## TERROIR

The vineyard is in one of the driest, sunniest pockets of England. The vineyard benefits from a strong coastal influence, low elevation and rich, free-draining clay soils making the site ideally suited for the production of quality sparkling and still wines. Sea breezes are key to their success, minimizing frost risk, reducing disease pressure and bringing a crisp salinity to their wines.

## ABOUT

Classically made English still and sparkling wines are grown in their coastal vineyards and produced by their small, dedicated team of winemakers in Herstmonceux, East Sussex. Henners vineyard was established in 2007.

## THE WINE

In the winery, Henners take a non-interventionist approach, made possible by the quality of the fruit. They have multiple vine clones and varieties planted to given them a broad palate of wines for final blending and play with reserve wines and oak barrels to contribute character, depth, richness and layers to their wines. Henners' wines are fermented and bottled on-site with their small, dedicated team responsible for every aspect of production.

### Henners Brut NV

Produced using the classical method, Henners Brut NV is a blend of the three classic sparkling grape varieties; Chardonnay, Pinot Noir and Pinot Meunier. Grown on both their own clay and grower's chalk soils which complement each other in terms of generosity and finesse. These components are blended each year with small proportions of reserve wine to bring additional depth and structure. Aged on lees for 3 years it is an elegant, refined wine with great balance and a delicious citrus and orchard fruit backbone.
Varieties: Chardonnay 40%, Pinot Noir 35%, Pinot Meunier 25%, Alcohol: 12%, Dosage: 7g/l

### Henners Rosé

Their Rosé NV is made from Pinot Noir and Pinot Meunier. Henners use the traditional saignée method to draw colour from the grapes at the pressing stage. Their Rosé delivers classic English Red berry fruit flavours including raspberries and redcurrants. A minimum of 18 months of ageing on the lees brings a delicate creaminess to the wine.
Varieties: Pinot Meunier 65%, Pinot Noir 35%. Alcohol: 12%. Dosage: 6.5 g/l

### Henners Vintage

Their vintage is crafted only in exceptional years, such as 2014, when they believe the concentration, ripeness and maturing of fruit will deliver an exceptional wine for extended ageing. Blended from 70% Chardonnay and 30% Pinot Noir, the Chardonnay delivers excellent structure and vibrancy, while the Pinot Noir brings body and depth to deliver great roundness on the palate. Their vintage spends 4 years on lees before release creating deliciously biscuity, creamy, honey aromas with deliciously poised acidity and a hint of salinity
Varieties: Chardonnay 70%, Pinot noir 30%. Vintage: 2014. Alcohol: 12%. Dosage: 9 g/l.

### Fiennes by Henners Brut NV

As with their Henners Brut NV, Fiennes NV is a blend of the three classic varieties of Chardonnay, Pinot Noir and Pinot Meunier, grown on a combination of their own clay soils and neighbouring grower's chalk soils. The cuvée is produced using the classical method and aged on lees for 3 years making it an elegant wine, filled with refreshing citrus and orchard fruit characteristics.

The label for Fiennes NV takes its inspiration from the floorplan of the Hertsmonceux Castle, built in the 15th century by owner Sir Roger Fiennes, and which neighbours the vineyards at Henners.
Varieties: Chardonnay 40%, Pinot Noir 35%, Pinot Meunier 25%, Alcohol 12%, Dosage 7 g/l

## VISITING AND BUYING

Buy online at **www.hennersvineyard.co.uk**
**Telephone: 01323 832073**

# HIDDEN SPRING VINEYARD

## EAST SUSSEX

HIDDEN SPRING VINEYARD, VINES CROSS ROAD, EAST SUSSEX TN21 0HG

- 9 Ha **of planted vines**

- **Winemaker David McNally**

- **Vintage information First release 2015 Bacchus blend, Current wines: Sparkling wines from 2017 and 2018 released, Bacchus blends form 2018 and 2019 released and Pinot Gris from 2019, in cellar Sparkling Rosé from 2020 and sparkling wines from 2017,18,19,20 harvests.**

- **Grape varieties Bacchus, Pinot Gris, Chardonnay, Pinot Noir, Pinot Meunier, Cabernet Noir**

## TERROIR

Tunbridge Wells clay on greensand provides a relatively vigorous site with free draining sand below for the roots to find nutrients and moisture even in hot dry periods. The iron rich clays of the weald region have an impact on the wines which are bright and aromatic with good acidity, rich in fruit and complexity.

## ABOUT

Hidden Spring Vineyard is situated on a 9 Ha (23 acre) site in the village of Horam, near Heathfield in the heart of East Sussex. The vineyard was originally established in 1986 and experienced many years of successful, high-quality wine production, providing award-winning wines across the country.

In 2015 the current owners Chris and David took over the site and expanded the vineyard plantings with sparkling varietals, Bacchus and Pinot Gris. Further investment in 2018 saw the opening of the new on-site winery and the production of wine on site for the first time. A further planting in 2019 added Cabernet Noir to the portfolio. Winemaker David and Vineyard Manager Chris trained at Plumpton College switching careers in IT in London for viticulture in East Sussex. A steep learning curve combined with passion and keen attention to detail have delivered fabulous results.

Having seen success in competitions, achieving numerous awards for their still wines including from Decanter, IWC and WineGB, the newly released Classic Cuvée 2018 has already been awarded a Silver medal from IWC. Rosé and Blanc de Blancs wines are in the pipeline – the latter being aged for at least 5 years in cellar to maximise its potential.

Visitors to Hidden Spring can book on to a Tour and Tutored Wine Tasting experience, browse the current wines at the Cellar Door shop or enjoy a glass of wine outside overlooking the vines. A range of events take place throughout the year including Shakespeare performances, choral concerts and pop-up restaurant nights.

## THE WINE

### Classic Cuvée 2018

A traditional method classic cuvée sparkling wine. An explosion of lemon and lime, a hint of aniseed and aromas of cherry blossom excite the nose and palate. The rich texture and ripe Red fruit notes expressed in this classic blend reflect the near perfect growing conditions of 2018. Classic blend of Chardonnay, Pinot Noir and Meunier. 12% ABV, 75cl/bottle.

### Blanc de Noirs 2017

Traditional method sparkling wine. It is lively and bright with lemon peel, blackberry and brioche aromas leading to flavours of lime, blackcurrant and crunchy green apple, vibrant bubbles with a lingering finish make this a real gem. 100% Pinot Noir grapes, 12% ABV, 75cl/bottle.

## VISITING AND BUYING

Buy online at www.hiddenspring.co.uk/shop
Telephone: 01435 813078

# JENKYN PLACE

## HAMPSHIRE

HOLE LANE, BENTLEY, HAMPSHIRE GU10 5LU

- 5.4 Ha **of planted vines**

- 30,000 **bottles annually**

- **Winemaker Dermot Sugrue**

- **Vintage information Currently drinking 2010 Blanc de Noir, with youngest wine on sale being 2015 Blanc de Blancs**

- **Grape varieties Chardonnay, Pinot Noir, Pinot Meunier**

## TERROIR

The wines are the brainchild of Simon Bladon. He moved his family to Jenkyn Place in 1997 and, after extensive renovations, turned his thoughts to the abandoned hop fields next to the property.

Hops play an important part in their story as Jenkyn Place had been an award-winning hop farm for longer than the oldest local can remember. They believe that the same nutrients and soils which made such special sparkling beers are contributing to the aromas and flavours of their sparkling wines as well. The vineyards are located on sheltered, south-facing slopes, straddling the 100m (328 feet) contour of Hampshire's North Downs. The soil, greensand over marlstone, is perfectly suited to Champagne varieties.

## ABOUT

Jenkyn Place is a boutique, family-owned estate set in the idyllic Hampshire countryside. The vineyard was established in 2004 with excellence in mind and designed and planted to produce top quality wines. Specialising in dry single-vintage sparkling wine, it produces a Brut Cuvée, Rosé, Blanc de Blancs and a Blanc de Noir. These are made in the traditional method from classic grape varieties Chardonnay, Pinot Noir and Pinot Meunier.

Jenkyn Place itself is an impressive William and Mary Grade II listed building, dating from the 17th Century. Located in Bentley, it is where the owner of White Star Lines, Harold Sanderson learned of the sinking of the Titanic in 1912. While the history of Jenkyn Place may stretch back to the 17th century, its roots as a top-quality wine estate have a much more contemporary story to tell.

## THE WINE

Jenkyn Place's award-winning wines are distinctly and proudly English with a fascinating history, beautiful location, classic packaging and a family committed to nurturing the Jenkyn Place brand, synonymous with English excellence.

### Jenkyn Place Classic Cuvée 2014

Though this wine is 'fresh, fragrant and delicate', it has a 'core' which would be the envy of every Pilates/Yoga aficionado in the world. It is lively, has real vibrance, and it is fine-boned, elegant and precise. The 2014 is made of 60% Chardonnay (62% in 2013), with 25% Pinot Noir and 15% Pinot Meunier, so it shares many family characteristics of its 2013 sibling. This is the 9th Vintage from the 5.2 Ha (13 acres) now planted at Jenkyn Place.

### Jenkyn Place Sparkling Rosé 2014

This is no ordinary Rosé. It just bubbles with attitude, with aromas of freshly-baked brioche and preserved lemons, plus rosehip and redcurrant on the palate. Their Pinot Noir dominates this wine with its richness and chalk-meets-umami undertones. Finally, the Chardonnay arrives like

the cavalry, balancing the wines with its rapier-like freshness and floral elegance.

### Jenkyn Place Blanc de Noir 2010

This is a sparkling wine with complexity and depth – think cherries, almonds, baked rye bread, ripe limes. Its two Red grape varieties have been pressed so gently that not a trace of the colour of their skins has had time to enter the wine. Here, 1+1 equals 3, the Pinot Noir giving elegance and finesse, while its often unsung compatriot the Pinot Meunier acts as a backcloth for its friend, putting the Pinot Noir on the pedestal it so totally merits, and on to a tongue-tingling climax.

### Jenkyn Place Blanc de Blancs 2015

This Blanc de Blancs is made only from their vineyards' 8,500 Chardonnay vines. It is the first Blanc de Blancs they have ever made, and the 2015 Vintage, with its low yields and concentrated fruit, has given it weight and complexity. It is also beautifully fresh, with a sherbet explosion of lemon and verbena, plus Victoria plum and rich, ripe citrus.

## VISITING AND BUYING

Contact: Camilla Jennings Sales & Marketing Manager: camilla@jenkynplace.com
Telephone: 01420 481581
Mobile: 07825 161685
www.jenkynplace.com

# Spotlight on
# NYETIMBER

## WEST SUSSEX

GAY STREET, WEST CHILTINGTON, WEST SUSSEX RH20 2HH

NYETIMBER
PRODUCT OF ENGLAND

- **350 Ha** of vines planted across West Sussex, Hampshire and Kent
- **c.1 million** bottles annually
- **Winemakers** Cherie Spriggs (Head Winemaker), Brad Greatrix (Winemaker)
- **Inaugural Vintage** 1992
- **Grape varieties** Chardonnay, Pinot Noir and Pinot Meunier

## TERROIR

Comprising several individual sites, Nyetimber's estate owned vineyards are distinctive and truly special. Selected for their precise geographical location, geology and microclimate, their vines perfectly suit the greensand and chalk soils of West Sussex, Hampshire and Kent, and their setting on gentle, south-facing slopes. It is this entirely unique and harmonious balance of factors that contributes to the elegance, complexity and finesse for which their wines are renowned.

## ABOUT

For over 30 years, Nyetimber has had a single aim: crafting exceptional English Sparkling Wine that rivals the very best in the world. A true pioneer, Nyetimber was the first producer of English Sparkling Wine to exclusively grow the three celebrated grape varieties: Chardonnay, Pinot Noir and Pinot Meunier. Nyetimber's owner, Eric Heerema, introduced best practices from around the world and a dedication to excellence which has been fundamental in building Nyetimber into a world-class producer. Since 2007, Head Winemaker Cherie Spriggs and her Winemaker husband Brad Greatrix have individually assessed every handpicked parcel of grapes to ensure only the finest fruit goes into the creation of Nyetimber's wines. Made from one hundred percent estate-grown grapes, Nyetimber crafts all its wines according to the traditional method, ageing them for extended periods of time to build complexity and flavour, resulting in wines of extraordinary elegance and quality.

## THE WINE

### Classic Cuvee Multi-Vintage

Lovely pale gold and gentle, fine bubbles. Toasty, spicy and complex aromas showing wonderful development after extended ageing in their cellar (usually more than three years). The palate supports these complex aromas with honey, almond, pastry and baked apple flavours. Very fine and elegant with a great combination of intensity, delicacy and length.

### Blanc de Blancs 2013

Lovely pale gold in colour with a fine bead, this Blanc de Blancs is the essence of pure Chardonnay. The aromas and flavours are in perfect harmony, beginning with delicate floral and citrus followed by subtle vanilla and toast. A long, complex finish makes this a wine to be savoured.

### Rosé MV

Sunset pink in colour, aromas include a charming mix of fresh Red fruit and intriguing spice notes of anise and lavender. The palate has a creamy, round texture balanced with redcurrant, raspberry and cherry flavours. Suggestions of brioche lead into an elegant, silky finish.

### Cuvee Chérie Demi-Sec MV

Light golden hues and a slight silver undertone illuminate this delicately effervescent wine. Aromas of pure lemon, mineral and honey tones and a hint of tangerine fill the nose. The palate has a lively sweet lemon start set off by a crisp acidity and a very clean, pure structure. The finish is minerally and citrus-filled.

### Tillington Single Vineyard 2013

As the fine bubbles rise in this pale gold wine, aromas of wild strawberries and raspberries emerge, reminiscent of British summer fruits. On the palate this delicate fruit is accompanied by complex flavours of toasted almonds, pastry and praline. The wine balances elegance and richness in perfect harmony, with a refreshing acidity and textured, decadent finish.

### Nyetimber 1086 2010

England's finest Prestige Cuvees, 1086 wines are characterised by their balance; acidity, length and texture are all beautifully judged and combine seamlessly upon the palate. The 2010 vintage has alluring aromas including notes of honey, pastry and roasted nuts. A shimmering core of acidity carries the wine to a pure and long finish. The wine wraps around the palate in a slow reveal, and gains in intrigue as it sits in the glass.

### Nyetimber 1086 Rosé 2010

The 2010 vintage Rosé is silky and elegant with a pure crystalline backbone, evoking floral, cassis and Red fruit aromas. Wonderful progression, with great tension between fruit and structure and a persistent finish.

## VISITING AND BUYING

Details of estate open days and online purchases are available at **www.nyetimber.com**
**General Enquiries: Tel. 0207 734 8490**
**Email: info@nyetimber.com**

# OXNEY ORGANIC ESTATE

## EAST SUSSEX

OXNEY ORGANIC ESTATE, HOBBS LANE, BECKLEY, RYE TN31 6TU

- **14 Ha of planted vines**

- **38,00050,000 bottles annually**

- **Winemaker Salvatore Leone**

- **Grape varieties Pinot Noir, Pinot Meunier, Chardonnay, Seyval Blanc**

## TERROIR

Oxney is north of Rye on the south coast of England – 17 metres (55 feet) above sea level and six miles (9.6 km) from the English Channel. The vineyard is planted in five blocks and surrounds the winery which is located in an old oast house – a testament to the hop growing traditions of the area. From a south-west slope the vines stretch out in a bowl towards a wood with giant oak trees, creating a warm and protected microclimate. The topsoil is Tunbridge Wells Sand, a fine sand and silt loam, above clay. The organic viticulture practices use under vine hoeing and a natural regime to keep the vines healthy. The soil is the number one priority and every year farm-yard manure from a neighbouring farmer is spread under the vines.

## ABOUT

The vineyard at Oxney Organic Estate is located in the south east corner of East Sussex. The area is becoming a new wine region with vineyards planted along the old Rother river delta. The vineyard is part of the founders' – Kristin Syltevik and Paul Dobson – vision of modern farming that's environmentally sound, natural and sustainable. The estate is organic and certified by the Soil Association.

The organic system at Oxney produces healthy, balanced and natural fruit. This approach is replicated in the winery where the organic low intervention regime is focused around small batch winemaking where each variety and clone is pressed and fermented separately using wild yeast from the vineyard, a low intervention regime is followed by careful blending decisions.

## THE WINE

Oxney is focused on sparkling wine but also produces some still wines:

### Classic 2017

Made from Chardonnay, Pinot Noir and Pinot Meunier grapes hand-picked early, to mid-October 2017 from their Dobson and Thomson blocks. Each parcel was whole-bunch pressed and fermented separately. All wines underwent malolactic conversion; some were fermented and aged in old Burgundy barrels to add complexity. The base wines were blended and bottled for the second fermentation in February 2018, before spending a minimum of 24 months on lees and three months on cork prior to release. Dosage: 6g/L.

### Classic Rosé 2016

Made with 100% Pinot Noir this sparkling wine spent 29 months on lees. Pale copper-pink colour with a fine, persistent and delicate mousse. The nose is lifted, complex and showing some lovely autolytic development with savoury aromas of shortbread, fresh pastry and baked bread alongside crunchy Red berry fruits and Red apple skin, set against a backbone of salinity. The saline quality also comes through on the palate, with the 2016 showing a broad rich texture combined with tightly knit acidity. Flavours of wild strawberries, toast and hazelnut dominate a long, focused finish. Dosage 6 g/L.

### Classic Pinot Meunier 2017

They picked their Pinot Meunier from the Thomson block in October 2017, gently pressed the juice from whole bunches and fermented it in barrel for several weeks. Over that time they trialled bâtonnage to stir the lees and add complexity to the base wine. Bottled in June 2018, disgorged in October 2020 and released in a recently-disgorged style to promote full freshness and complexity. On the nose, the aromas flit seductively from cherries and frangipane to Christmas cake to heather honey through to nutty Edam cheese. The palate is clean and dry but unveils layers of soft Red cherry fruit, marzipan, toast and kirsch. The texture drifts elusively from tangy to creamy in the course of a single sip. Dosage: 5g/L.

### Classic Chardonnay 2017

Chardonnay picked from their Thomson and Dobson blocks on the 11 October 2017. This is their first vintage Chardonnay English Sparkling Wine. 100% Chardonnay, so in essence a blanc de blancs. Fermented in old barrels. A refined and precise wine, citrus and brioche notes. Dosage: 5.5g/L.

## VISITING AND BUYING

Open by appointment all year round.
Book on www.oxneyestate/vineyard-tours
Or buy online: www.oxneyestate.com/shop or www.oxneyestate.com/stockists/
Or just stop by the shop April – October open Saturday 10am – 4pm.
Oxney has extensive accommodation:
www.oxneyestate.com/stay
Contact details:
Telephone: 01797 260137
Email: wine@oxneyestate.com

# Spotlight on
# PLUMPTON ESTATE WINES

## EAST SUSSEX

PLUMPTON COLLEGE, DITCHLING ROAD, PLUMPTON, EAST SUSSEX, BN7 3AE

- 10 Ha of planted vines
- 25,000 bottles annually
- Winemakers Deepika Koushik and Sarah Midgley
- Grape varieties Chardonnay, Pinot Noir and Pinot Meunier

## TERROIR

Rock Lodge Vineyard was established over 50 years ago on gently sloping southern facing slopes that allow maximum sunshine for the vines and provide cold air drainage to minimise frosts. Vines have their roots in 20 to 50 cm (8 to 19.5 in) of clay loam over the top of sandstone and this allows for some natural vigour control and well managed Chardonnay, Pinot Noir and Pinot Meunier which produces excellent fruit for traditional method sparkling wine and traditional method brut Rosé.

## ABOUT

The award-winning Plumpton Estate sparkling wines are produced by their enthusiastic and talented students, working alongside a team of vine growing and winemaking experts. Welcoming students from all over the world, Plumpton College is the UK's Centre of Excellence in Education, Training and Research offering degrees from level 4–7, all validated by the Royal Agricultural University, a level 3 viticulture apprenticeship and Wine Skills program. As well as vineyards and a commercial winery, Plumpton Wine Division also boasts a research centre, laboratories, and a sensory evaluation room. Plumpton Wine Division is the only institute in Europe to offer this level of academic and vocational education, all taught in the English language.

## THE WINE

### Plumpton Estate Brut Classic NV
Classic Sparkling Brut

Dry, with refreshing acidity and delicate fine yet persistent mousse. This wine displays complex crisp apple and citrus fruit notes perfectly balanced with creamy brioche roundness and a long refreshing finish. Quality English Sparkling Wine at its finest.

### Plumpton Estate Brut Rosé NV
Sparkling Rosé

Dry and youthful with a fine and creamy persistent mousse. This wine has an appealing salmon pink blush hue and displays delicate cherry and green apple fruit with floral hints well balanced with a soft yeasty body.

### VISITING AND BUYING:

Please contact Plumpton Estate Wine Division on 01273 892128 or winesales@plumpton.ac.uk for all visitor enquires and orders.

# Spotlight on
# RATHFINNY WINE ESTATE

## EAST SUSSEX

RATHFINNY WINE ESTATE, ALFRISTON, EAST SUSSEX, BN26 5TU

RATHFINNY

- **93 Ha** of planted vines with 380,000 vines planted
- **Owners** Mark and Sarah Driver
- **Grape varieties** Pinot Noir, Chardonnay and Meunier

## TERROIR

Rathfinny Wine Estate is located in Sussex, England. Their soil type is silty clay loam soil over chalk, providing free-draining soil.

## ABOUT

A family-owned Wine Estate, established in 2010 by Mark and Sarah Driver, dedicated to producing some of the world's finest sparkling wines from a single-site vineyard in Sussex, England. Located on a wonderful south-facing slope in England's South Downs, chalk soil, climate, and aspect make it the perfect site.

## THE WINE

Rathfinny winemaking philosophy: their low-intervention, traditional method, vintage Sussex Sparkling wines are a true expression of their terroir. Produced from hand-harvested grapes that are whole-bunch pressed and patiently matured, on lees and in bottle to develop rich, autolytic notes, with a low dosage that emphasises the purity of their fruit.

Four principal Sussex Sparkling wines produced, all vintage: Classic Cuvée, their 'house-style' sparkling – blend of Pinot Noir, Chardonnay and Meunier. Rosé, their expressive sparkling – Pinot Noir dominated. Blanc de Blancs, their elegant

sparkling – Pure Chardonnay. Blanc de Noirs, their signature sparkling – blend of Pinot Noir and Meunier.

### 2016 BLANC DE NOIRS
Rathfinny Blanc de Noirs 2016 is the second vintage of their signature blend which is predominately Pinot Noir grapes, which are hand-harvested and the wine is aged for 36 months in the bottle.

### 2016 BLANC DE BLANCS
Rathfinny Blanc de Blancs 2016 is the second vintage of their popular sparkling wine, produced from a blend of predominately Burgundy clones of Chardonnay, which are hand-harvested and

the wine is aged for 36 months in the bottle.

### 2017 ROSÉ BRUT

Rathfinny Rosé Brut 2017 is the third vintage of their popular Pinot Noir dominated Sussex sparkling wine, with a red-fruit style that beautifully showcases the increased presence of Pinot Noir within the blend. Aged for 24 months in the bottle.

### 2016 CLASSIC CUVÉE

Their first vintage of their Classic Sussex Sparkling is made from a blend of predominantly Pinot Noir with Chardonnay and Pinot Meunier, aged for 36 months in the bottle.

## VISITING AND BUYING

Visit Rathfinny for wine tours and tastings at the Cellar Door, dining in the Tasting Room and Flint Barns restaurant, stay a night in the Flint Barns or to host a special event with us. Please check the website for visitor information.
**https://rathfinnyestate.com/**

*Spotlight on*
# RIDGEVIEW WINE ESTATE

## EAST SUSSEX

RIDGEVIEW WINE ESTATE, FRAGBARROW LANE, DITCHLING COMMON, EAST SUSSEX BN6 8TP

- **Area** Ridgeview source from 101 Ha (250 acres) across Hampshire, Sussex, Kent, Essex, Suffolk
- **Production** Ridgeview 400,000
- **Director of Winemaking** Simon Roberts
- **Vintage information** Blanc de Blanc, Blanc de Noir, Rosé de Noir
- **Grape varieties** Chardonnay, Pinot Noir, Pinot Meunier

## TERROIR

Ridgeview's original vineyards are situated a mile north of Ditchling Beacon in the South Downs National Park, planted in a clay loam soil above a limestone ridge, the highest point of the vineyard is 60m (197 ft) above sea level, 13 km (eight miles) north of the sea. Each of these factors have an influence on the characteristic and flavours of the fruit. Since this original planting they now source fruit from over 100 hectares (247 acres) all over the south of England; from Suffolk and Essex through to Kent, Sussex and Hampshire. Each region brings something different to the table. When it comes to blending each year, they have a vast selection of different wines to choose from. Their Blanc de Blanc is the only single estate wine, while their Bloomsbury, their largest blend may have over 60 components. One barrel from Essex may have a dramatic effect on a blend.

## HISTORY

Ridgeview have been at the forefront of crafting traditional method English Sparkling Wines since 1995. Nestled at the foot of the South Downs, the second-generation family company were one of the first English wineries to solely concentrate on growing Chardonnay, Pinot Noir and Pinot Meunier. Over 20 years since foundation, production has increased to more than a quarter of a million bottles and Ridgeview is sold across the world. At the helm

is CEO Tamara Roberts and her brother, Simon Roberts, is Director of Winemaking.

Ridgeview have been served at a collection of Royal occasions including State Banquets for President Obama and President Xi Jingping, and are winners of numerous international accolades, including 'Winemaker of the Year' IWSC. The vineyard was also recently crowned number 36 in the 'Top 50 World's Best Vineyards'.

Ridgeview's dedication, passion and determination have significantly contributed to the international reputation of English Sparkling Wine, leading the way in exporting to 17 countries globally.

## ABOUT

Ridgeview has expanded greatly since the first planting in 1995; originally producing 20,000 bottles, they have grown steadily to producing over 400,000 bottles, and continued expansion should see Ridgeview make 600,000 bottles by 2025. Their newly finished production facility gives them the capability to cope with the growth. Underground cellars in the original winery and the new building means that they can store up to 1 million bottles without requiring temperature control which helps to support their focus on sustainability.

As well as their Ridgeview wines they also make wines for Waitrose, Marks and Spencer's, Laithwaites, Booths and the Wine Society, as well

as contract winemaking for numerous clients. In total they make over 35 Cuvées.

With a team of 33 people, Ridgeview strives to produce some of the best sparkling wines in the world. As pioneers of the English Sparkling Wine industry it has always been important to Ridgeview to lead the way be it in the quality and style of their wines, to their sustainability as a business and to position their brand both domestically and internationally. In 2018 Ridgeview went through a complete re-branding; moving from their 1920s inspired labelling, evoking the decadence and opulence of the time to a more modern, crisp, contemporary branding; cementing their position at the forefront of the industry.

2020 was their 25th anniversary, and to celebrate they released a Ridgeview oak-aged barrel fermented sparkling wine.

## SIGNATURE WINES

### BLOOMSBURY NV
Their signature blend Bloomsbury is light golden in colour with a fine, persistent mousse. Citrus fruit aromas with hints of melon and honey. Chardonnay dominance brings finesse, along with crisp freshness. The Pinots add depth and character leading to a beautifully balanced finish. This will age gracefully over time as the Chardonnay matures.

### CAVENDISH NV
Their traditional blend Cavendish is a rich golden colour with exceptionally fine bubbles. The nose is expressive with hints of Red fruits. The Pinot

dominance brings depth and complexity to the palate with a long-lasting finish, while the Chardonnay adds finesse and freshness.

### FITZROVIA NV
Their Fitzrovia Rosé is a delicate salmon colour with an abundance of fine bubbles. Chardonnay brings freshness and finesse, while the Pinots add the classic Red fruits for which England is so acclaimed. A raspberry and redcurrant nose carries through to a fresh fruit-driven palate.

## LIMITED RELEASES

### BLANCE DE BLANC (VINTAGE)
Pure Chardonnay from their original Ditchling vineyard. Concentrated, fresh and precise. Gold medal winner in the International Wine Challenge 2018.

### BLANC DE NOIR (VINTAGE)
Finest Pinot Noir and Pinot Meunier from the very best vintages. These varieties produce a rich, robust and earthy flavour, reflective of their cool climate with great complexity and texture. Gold medal winner in The Glass of Bubbly Awards 2018.

### ROSÈ DE NOIR (VINTAGE)
Rare Saignée-method Rosé from the ripest Pinot Noir and Meunier. A complex, textural Rosé. Gold medal winner in Champagne & Sparkling Wine World Championships 2018.

### OAK RESERVE
Made over several vintages and aged in a careful selection of new and old Oak barrels, using 100% Chardonnay, buttery and vanilla on the nose, lychees and pineapple on the palate.

## AWARDS

### WINEMAKER OF THE YEAR
Further global accolades:
www.ridgeview.co.uk/awards/

## VISITING AND BUYING
Email: Retail@ridgeview.co.uk
Telephone: 01444 242040

# ROEBUCK ESTATES

## WEST SUSSEX

ROEBUCK ESTATES, UPPERTON FARM, TILLINGTON, PETWORTH, GU28 0RD

- 50 Ha **of planted vines**

- **100,000** bottles annually

- Winemaker **Emma Rice**

- Vintage information **Classic Cuvée 2014, Blanc de Noirs 2015, Rosé de Noirs 2016**

- Grape varieties **Chardonnay, Pinot Noir, Pinot Meunier**

### TERROIR

The vineyards that make up Roebuck Estates span the width of the beautiful county of Sussex. Situated close to the picturesque market town of Petworth in West Sussex lies the Roebuck vineyard which is the jewel in their crown and home to their oldest vines planted back in 2006. With its magnificent southerly views of the South Downs and rolling hills, their 'home' vineyard has the ideal terroir for growing the classic sparkling grape varieties of Chardonnay, Pinot Noir and Pinot Meunier destined for their sparkling wines.

### ABOUT

Roebuck Estates was established in 2013 by two Brits whose love of wine, long-standing friendship and belief in the potential of the English wine industry sparked several years spent searching for and establishing the perfect vineyard plots across Sussex. Since the debut release of their Classic Cuvée in 2019, Roebuck Estates has won numerous trophies and gold medals in prestigious UK and international wine competitions and has quickly earned a reputation as a producer of quality sparkling wines. The team at Roebuck Estates are also incredibly proud to be one of the founding members of the Sustainable Wines of Great Britain certification scheme.

## THE WINE

### Classic Cuvée 2014

A rich, yet refined sparkling wine displaying a wonderful balance of elegance and finesse. Crafted from a harmonious blend of Chardonnay, Pinot Noir and Pinot Meunier, only the very best fruit is carefully selected and harvested by hand for their flagship wine. Delightful notes of citrus fruit and baked apples are layered with a toasty richness and delicious hint of truffle leading to a long, balanced finish. 'Best in Show' winner at the Decanter World Wine Awards 2020.

### Blanc de Noirs 2015

A single-estate release crafted exclusively from Pinot Noir grapes grown at their Roman Villa vineyard. The fruit was carefully hand-picked and partially fermented in the finest Burgundian oak barrels followed by a generous period of bottle-ageing for a minimum of four years. This is a wonderfully complex wine with delicate bubbles, a silky texture and a long-lingering finish. Baked apples and ripe stone fruits on the palate are layered with notes of brioche and toasted almonds.

### Rosé de Noirs 2016

An elegant sparkling Rosé made from perfectly ripe estate-grown Pinot Noir grapes. Carefully hand-selected fruit was gently whole-bunch pressed and partially fermented in the finest Burgundian oak barrels. A splash of Pinot Précoce was added prior to release imparting a delicate

pink hue and pretty wild red berry notes. This is a beautifully balanced wine displaying fragrant notes of wild strawberries, white peach and a hint of honeysuckle. 'English Vintage Sparkling Rosé' Trophy winner at the International Wine Challenge 2021.

## VISITING AND BUYING

General Enquiries:
Email: hello@roebuckestates.co.uk
Telephone: 01798 263123
www.roebuckestates.co.uk

# SIMPSONS' WINE ESTATE

## KENT

SIMPSONS' WINE ESTATE, THE BARNS, CHURCH LANE, BARHAM, NR CANTERBURY, KENT, CT4 6PB

- **30 Ha of planted vines**
- **250,000 bottles annually**
- **Winemakers Ruth & Charles Simpson**
- **Consultant Oenologist Leigh Sparrow**
- **Vintage information 2016**
- **Grape varieties Pinot Noir, Pinot Meunier and Chardonnay**

## TERROIR

Simpsons' Wine Estate is situated amid the pristine beauty of the Elham Valley – an unspoilt seam in the North Downs of Kent where the contours of the land, the climate and the soil could scarcely be improved upon for viticulture.

The intensely lime-rich chalk soil, forming part of the same chalk ridge that stretches from southern England to the French Champagne and Burgundy regions, is perfect for the cultivation of Pinot Noir, Pinot Meunier and Chardonnay, the time-honoured trio of grapes that create the world's finest sparkling wines and also some of the best still wines. The English climate may be marginal for viticulture but the resulting wines show elegance, finesse and impressive ageing potential, thanks to a long, cool ripening period.

## ABOUT

Ruth and Charles Simpson have been making award-winning wines at Domaine de Sainte Rose, their stunning, southern French property, since 2002. In 2012, attracted by the quality of the terroir and the opportunity to join one of the most dynamic wine producing regions of the world, Ruth and Charles brought their expertise and savoir-faire back to the UK, establishing Simpsons' Wine Estate with an aspiration to produce the finest quality English wines.

2016 saw the inaugural harvest for the Estate, with Oz Clarke opening the state-of-the-art winery, located mere moments from the vines. Since then the winemakers have produced a highly-acclaimed range of exclusively estate-grown still and sparkling wines. In 2020 Simpsons' Wine Estate was named as a Walpole Brand of Tomorrow, heralding the company's arrival as a recognised emerging British luxury brand.

The summer months provide opportunities for visitors to explore the glorious vineyards and to enjoy guided tasting events in the elegant Glass House Tasting Room, which overlooks the winery. Moreover, Simpsons' Wine Estate boasts the unique attraction of a helter-skelter from the tasting room to the winery, ensuring their events finish with an unforgettable flourish down the 'Fruit Chute' slide!

## THE WINE

The flawless combination of savoir-faire, perfect vineyard sites, meticulous farming and impeccable winemaking has resulted in the creation of a range of premium still and sparkling wines at Simpsons' Wine Estate. The ability to produce world class still wine has been particularly rewarding for the Estate. With a strong emphasis on provenance and exuding a true sense of place, these exceptional wines are designed to challenge the perception of English wines both nationally and internationally. Highlights of the Simpsons' Wine Estate collection include:

### Chalklands Classic Cuvée

Created from estate grown Chardonnay and Pinot

Noir grapes, this classic cuvée is the epitome of English elegance. The very first vintage of this English Sparkling Wine, Chalklands Classic Cuvée 2016, garnered a Gold Medal and 'Best in Class' title in the 2019 Champagne and Sparkling Wine World Championships.

### Flint Fields Blanc de Noirs

This premium Classic Method Blanc de Noirs is top of the Simpsons' range and exemplifies English finesse and balance. Created from estate grown Pinot Noir Clone 115 grapes, this particular variety was selected to create a more full-bodied style owing to a slight accentuation of tannins, which develop a more luxurious mouth-feel. This effortlessly elegant Blanc de Noirs won a Gold Medal in the 2020 International Wine Challenge.

### Canterbury Rosé Sparkling Rosé 2018

Aged for 15 months on lees, Canterbury Rosé is delicately pink with a fine mousse and a soft bouquet of rose petal and strawberry sorbet. A creamy, rounded texture is balanced with crisp berry flavours and a refined finish.

## VISITING AND BUYING

**Visit www.simpsonwine.com to book on to their Tour and Tasting events.**
**General Enquiries: Tel: 01227 832200**
**Email: info@simpsonswine.com**
**Press Enquiries: helen@simpsonswine.com**

# TERLINGHAM VINEYARD

## KENT

TERLINGHAM VINEYARD, TERLINGHAM LANE, HAWKINGE CT18 7AE

- 1.6 Ha **of planted vines**

- 2,000–4,000 **bottles per year**

- **Winemaker** Defined Wines

- **Vintage information** Blanc de Noir 2015

- **Grape varieties** Bacchus, Rhondo, Doornfelder, Pinot Noir, Pinot Meunier and Chardonnay

## TERROIR

Terlingham Vineyard is located on a gorgeous south-facing slope just outside of Folkestone on the Kent North Downs, with fabulous views over the Channel to France. The lovely sea breezes help to prevent frost and, being so close to Dover, the vines are on chalky soil with excellent drainage.

## ABOUT

Terlingham Vineyard is a sustainable, boutique vineyard, producing unique artisanal wines. They are small but mighty! With just four acres of vines, they make between 2,000 and 4,000 bottles of wine a year. Terlingham are all about being as low impact, sustainable and eco-friendly as possible in everything they do, both on the vineyard and when they make their wines. Their family of five does everything on the vineyard themselves, by hand.

Terlingham use natural farming techniques, which means that they don't use any artificial fertilisers, pesticides or herbicides. Because of this, each harvest produces exciting, varied and award-winning wines, each one with a unique character and its own story.

They are delighted to partner with Owen Elias and the fabulous team at Defined Wines to make their wines.

All of their labels are eco-friendly. They are paper based rather than plastic, and they do not use foil toppers on their sparkling wines – they have replaced this with a paper tab.

## THE WINE

### 2016 Natural Sparkling Rosé

This vibrant sparkling wine was fermented naturally and has no added dosage. Made from the noble Champagne blend of Chardonnay, Pinot Noir and Pinot Meunier, the wine boasts a lovely soft rose colour. Delightfully crisp apple on the nose, and bright flavours of redcurrant and raspberry on the palate. Vegan friendly. 10% alcohol.

### 2015 Natural Sparkling White

This wine was fermented naturally and has no added dosage, creating an exciting and extra brut sparkling wine. This Blanc de Noir is a blend of Pinot Noir and Pinot Meunier which showcases a soft golden colour and persistent bubbles in the glass. With vibrant aromas of melon on the nose, it is wonderfully crisp on the palate with flavours of green apple, pear and melon. Beautifully balanced with a long finish. Awarded a bronze IEWA awarded in 2019. Vegan friendly. 10% alcohol.

### 2012 Sparkling White

Pinot Noir, Pinot Meunier and Chardonnay grapes combine beautifully in this delicate and enjoyable brut sparkling wine. Showcasing a colour blend of White gold with abundant fine bubbles and soft aromas of fresh cut grass and apple. Wonderfully crisp on the palate with flavours of White and yellow flowers, peaches and nectarines which blend with a pleasant biscuitiness. 12.5% alcohol.

### 2012 Sparkling Rosé

Delightfully decadent, this sparkling Rosé wine is perfect for sharing with friends. Made from the honourable Champagne blend of Chardonnay, Pinot Noir and Pinot Meunier, the wine boasts a lovely pomegranate pink colour and a gentle, persistent, stream of bubbles. Delicate aromas of berries and candied orange peel, with a hint of brioche, play on the nose, with soft raspberry and strawberry flavours on the palate and a long finish. 12.5% Alcohol.

## VISITING AND BUYING

Terlingham love sharing their passion for natural farming (and their delicious wines)! They run vineyard tours and wine tastings by appointment throughout the year.
**Please call 01303 892452 or email contact@terlinghamvineyard.co.uk**

# TINWOOD ESTATE

## WEST SUSSEX

TINWOOD FARM, HALNAKER, CHICHESTER, WEST SUSSEX PO18 0NE

- 40 Ha **of planted vines**

- 50,000 **bottles annually**

- **Winemaker Simon Roberts (Ridgeview)**

- **Vintage information Blanc de Blanc 2017, Brut 2017, Rosé 2017**

- **Grape varieties Chardonnay, Pinot Noir, Pinot Meuniere**

## TERROIR

Tinwood Estate grow their vines on gravel soils based over chalk at the foot of the South Downs. They are approximately 4.8 km (3 miles) from the sea which protects them from frost and they sit in the rain shadow of the Isle of Wight to the South West of the vineyard. A fantastic place to grow top quality sparkling wine varieties.

## ABOUT

This second generation farmer has converted the farm from Iceberg lettuce to vines. After doing a vintage in New Zealand, Art (the owner) planted the first vines in 2007. Having always lived on the farm they have a connection and understanding with the soil and through experience built up over decades know which parts of the farm suit which variety.

They have subsequently expanded the vineyard a number of times and utilise the most modern growing techniques with the constant personal drive to produce the best quality grapes possible.

## THE WINE

### Blanc de Blanc 2017

A delicate pale gold with silvery highlights. Persistent bubbles giving an exceptional mousse. The bouquet is subtle with a suggestion of honey and brioche which will become more noticeable with ageing. The palate has a firm attack which makes this wine truly refreshing, with green apple and White tropical fruits in abundance. A beautifully balanced clean finish that lingers for a moment.

### Tinwood Estate Brut

Pale gold in colour with a lovely mousse and a fine stream of bubbles. Aromas of citrus melon fruits with hints of toast and honey. Fresh fruit flavours continue on the palate with depth and refinement added by the Pinots while the Chardonnay brings a freshness and finesse for which England is so acclaimed.

### Tinwood Estate Rosé

A gorgeous salmon colour with an abundance of bubbles and a beautifully creamy mousse. A raspberry and redcurrant nose with hints of strawberries and cream carry through to a delightfully fruit driven palate. Ideally suited while enjoying a glorious summer evening.

## VISITING AND BUYING

Tasting room is open every day of the year between 9am to 5.30pm conducting vineyard tours, overnight accommodation and wine sales. Visit www.tinwoodestate.com or email info@tinwoodestate.com

# Spotlight on
# WISTON ESTATE WINERY

## WEST SUSSEX

WISTON ESTATE WINERY, NORTH FARM, WASHINGTON, WEST SUSSEX RH20 4BB

- **10 Ha** of planted vines
- **80,000** bottles annually
- **Winemaker** Dermot Sugrue
- **Vintage information** Wiston produces 4 vintage wines Cuvée (their inaugural vintage was 2008), Blanc de Blancs (first vintage was 2010), Rosé (first vintage was 2011), Blanc de Noirs (first vintage was 2010)
- **Grape varieties** Chardonnay, Pinot Noir, Pinot Meunier

## TERROIR

Wiston's vines are planted on the South Downs in West Sussex on an escarpment of pure ancient chalk seam covered by a shallow layer (1030 cm/3.911.8 in) of topsoil. A natural sun-trap and protected from prevailing winds, the south-facing vineyard slope benefits from maximum sun exposure, promoting ripening.

Moderate rainfall, cool winters and temperate summers couple with cool breezes from the south coast, allowing the grapes to ripen slowly but fully and retain the crucial acidity and freshness vital to produce high-quality sparkling wine.

As in so many areas producing wines of outstanding quality, it is the chalky soil that imparts the complex flavours and structural elegance to the grapes and the wine itself.

## ABOUT

Nestled in the heart of England's rolling South Downs in West Sussex, the beautiful Wiston Estate has been in the hands of the Goring family since 1743 and is presided over today by Harry and Pip Goring. The estate is managed by their son Richard and both he and his wife, Kirsty, are now involved in the day to day running of the vineyard and winery. Pip's long-held vision was to plant vines on the estate and the original 6.5 ha (16 acre)

vineyard, which was planted in 2006, is the fruit of her dream and tenacity. With winemaker Dermot Sugrue at the helm, the team produces award-winning English Sparkling wines of exceptional purity and finesse from Chardonnay, Pinot Noir and Pinot Meunier.

The Estate believes in sustainable viticulture, using natural methods to optimise health and balance in the vineyard. Everything from pruning, to canopy management, to harvest, is all carried out by hand.

## THE WINE

### Wiston Brut NV

Made up of equal parts of Chardonnay, Pinot Noir and Pinot Meunier, their house style combines youthful purity of fruit with more mature characters from long lees-ageing. Refreshing, elegant and complete, with a complex finish, it was awarded a Master Medal at the 2021 Drinks Business Masters.

### Wiston Estate Cuvée 2015

Released with 4 years on the lees, this blend of 45% Pinot Noir, 33% Chardonnay and 22% Pinot Meunier shows impressive depth and complexity, while retaining Wiston's signature precision and elegance. Made only in the very best years, this

is the 5th vintage of their flagship wine and was awarded a Gold Medal in the WineGB Awards 2020.

### Wiston Estate Blanc de Blancs 2015
Selected from the chalkiest and steepest part of Wiston's vineyard, their vintage Blanc de Blancs is elegant and expressive, with enticing notes of tangerine, honeydew melon, honeysuckle and brioche. Described by wine critic Neal Martin as 'the best English Sparkling Wine I have tasted thus far', this decadent single vineyard, single vintage, single varietal Blanc de Blancs is perfect for immediate drinking and will also age beautifully. It was awarded the Wine GB Blanc de Blancs Trophy in 2021.

### Wiston Estate Rosé 2014
Comprised of 68% Pinot Noir, 22% Pinot Meunier and just 10% Chardonnay, their vintage Rosé wine displays exotic notes of Seville oranges, cranberries, morello cherries and sweet spice. There is extraordinary complexity and great texture due to two-thirds of this Cuvée being fermented and aged in oak barrels.

'One of my all-time favourite English Sparkling Wines, it doesn't get much better than this.' Adrian Smith, The Independent February 2018.

### Wiston Estate Cuvée 2013 Magnum
Released with 5 years on the lees and a further year on cork, this wine has an abundance of

fragrant English orchard fruits, honey, brioche, toasted hazelnuts, ginger and an underlying savoury minerality. Only 1,000 magnums were made of this limited release, which in 75cl format was awarded 'Best UK Sparkling Wine' in the Decanter World Wine Awards 2017, the English Sparkling Wine Trophy in the International Wine & Spirit Competition 2017 and selected by *Decanter* Magazine to be in their Top 25 Most Exciting Wines in the World 2017.

## VISITING AND BUYING

Tours and tastings can be booked online. The new winery and cellar door will open in November 2021, along with the restaurant, Chalk.

www.wistonestate.co.uk
General Enquiries:
winery@wistonestate.co.uk
Sales Enquiries:
sales@wistonestate.co.uk
Press Enquiries: Tori Eeles
tori@wistonestate.co.uk
Telephone: 01903 877845

# EAST ANGLIA

East Anglia offers the driest weather conditions in England, in combination with more sunlight and south-facing hills, creating favourable conditions for vines to grow. The Bacchus variety particularly thrives in this region, as well as Pinot Noir, so you can expect to enjoy elegant and aromatic wines that are internationally acclaimed.

Chet Valley Vineyard

Valley Farm
Vineyards

hilford Hall
Vineyard

Giffords Hall
Vineyard

West Street Vineyard

New Hall Vineyards

# Spotlight on
# CHET VALLEY VINEYARD

## NORFOLK

LODDON ROAD, BERGH APTON, NORWICH NORFOLK NR15 1BT

CHET
VALLEY
VINEYARD

- **10 Ha** of planted vines
- **8,000** bottles annually (2021) rising to **20,000 in the next three years**
- **Winemaker** John Hemmant
- **Vintage information** Horatio Brut, Skylark Brut, Red Kite Brut
- **Grape varieties** Solaris, Phoenix, Seyval Blanc, Regent, Chardonnay, Pinot Noir, Pinot Meuniere, Cabernet Noir, Sauvingon Blanc, Schoenburger

## TERROIR

The Hemmant family have held the land in Chet Valley since the beginning of the century. Fred Hemmant, John's great uncle, maintained a stable of horses which has imbued the soil with great organic content. Deeper down, the soil is sandy loam, gravel and pure sand. Below this is boulder clay. This terroir offers the grapes a well-drained soil that curbs excessive leaf formation and allows a loose soil structure perfect for worm activity and root formation. Each vine has a tap root that eventually hits the boulder clay, offering nutrition and an ample source of water for the vine.

The East Anglian climate offers purging frosts in the periods of dormancy over winter, which allows for the killing of vine diseases. In contrast, its summers bring more sunshine and higher temperatures than the rest of the UK on average, allowing the vineyard's grapes to ripen well, with vintages very often determined by the weather in September and October. The area is prone to Indian Summers, giving high sugar and aromaticity in the grapes, with low disease pressure.

## ABOUT

John Hemmant is a graduate chemist and proprietor vigneron, using a combination of influences of the new world winemakers and researchers, (particularly Professor Amerine of Davis University California) and old-world winemaking wisdom gained from numerous visits to winemakers of Germany, France and Italy. A true enthusiast, he periodically attends courses at the Plumpton Wine College to keep up with the latest techniques and developments in the wine industry. John is constantly seeking new innovative techniques in winemaking and recently produced a red sparkling wine called Red Kite using secondary fermentation in the bottle, the Great British Classic method. This has become a very popular wine which is made from the Regent grape pairing well with red meats, game and poultry.

## THE WINE

With grape varieties planted at Chet Valley Vineyard including Solaris, Phoenix, Schönburger, Chardonnay, and Seyval Blanc grown alongside Reds such as Pinot Noir, Pinot Meuniere, Cabernet Noir, Regent, Rondo and Dornfelder using traditional techniques optimised to their British terroir, the bottle collections prove truly unique to the location and are available for delivery nationwide. Chet Valley Wines are named after the birds that fly above the vineyard, Skylark, Siskin, Swift, Redwing, Red Kite, and Stone Chat. From the award-winning Charmat-style 'Skylark' wines and flagship wine 'Horatio' made in the Great British Classic method (similar to Champagne), to the varietal stills and 'Redwing' Regent Rosé, there's a bottle in Chet Valley's range to suit every palette.

## Skylark 2017

Fabulously fun, great party drink for everyone which has been commended in 2019 by both the Decanter World Wine Awards and the International Wine Challenge (IWC). Enjoy chilled on any celebration day.

## Skylark 2018

Award winning Skylark Brut Blush 2018 sparkling wine made using the Charmat Method. The Brut and demi sec sparkling wines are made from 80% Phoenix, 15% Seyval Blanc and 5% Regent grapes. Inspired by the melodious little birds that soar above the vines at Chet Valley Vineyard. The wines are light, bubbly and fruity. The demi sec goes particularly well with desserts and pastries.

## Horatio Pink sparkling wine

Great to drink on its own or with canapes. Clear, salmon pink in colour with a good mousse. Fruity aromatics with complex flavours and buttery, biscuity notes. A great wine for weddings and special birthdays.

## Red Kite

Red Kite is an exciting new sparkling Red wine on limited release from Chet Valley Vineyard. Initially available to lease holders and club members, now on general sale to everyone! Explosive bouquet of secondary fermentation is evidenced on the mousse. The wine has great bubbles, aromas of cranberry and cherry, light tannins and a good length. A great fun filled celebratory wine.

## Skylark Demi Sec

Their Charmat method sparkling Skylark Demi Sec 2018 vintage is a light Rosé sparkling, full of character with fruit aromatics of apple, lime, white peach, apricot, pear and tropical fruits. Made in south Norfolk from a blend of 80% Phoenix, 15% Seyval Blanc and 5% Regent grapes. Inspired by the melodious little birds that rise above the stunning permaculture on the Norfolk vineyard, Skylark is a great celebratory drink on its own but goes particularly well with desserts and cake. A magnificent aperitif.

## VISITING AND BUYING

Opening Times: Wine Sales at the wine cellar door – 10AM–5PM. Year-round Monday to Friday Including Bank Holidays. Open Saturdays from April to 30th September. Always Closed Sundays.

Chet Valley Vineyard welcomes visitors to the vineyard for tours and wine tastings, providing a safe outdoor experience for people to explore and learn more about vine growing, wine making and wine tasting plus food pairing. The tours are inclusive of young and old although wine tasting is strictly for the over 18s. Families are welcome to visit and spend some time relaxing together. The vineyard encourages the involvement of those with accessibility issues, hearing loss or sight loss and offers a true sensory experience for all. Luxury picnics on the vineyard can be booked in advance and there is a large indoor reception area on the first floor with a balcony overlooking the vineyard which is perfect for events and meetings, business away days etc. Additionally, there is an accessible holiday cottage amongst the vines called the Vine House which is all on one floor with no steps or slopes but with wide access doors. Chet Valley

Vineyard encourages involvement from villagers and friends with the harvest in the late summer. This sociable event gets everyone outdoors in the fresh air but with social interaction naturally distanced by the vine rows. Once the grapes are safely gathered, there is a harvest supper for all with flowing wine.

Chet Valley vineyard has a Wine Guild where members receive quarterly deliveries of award-winning wines in the format of a wine subscription. Within 1 year, the Head Winemaker carefully composes and sends out 4 mixed cases of artisan wine, with each containing three bottles. Deliveries occur in February, May, August and November. Guild members receive a 10% discount on all wines and Chet Valley event tickets purchased within your membership period. In addition complementary admittance to:-
1) All harvest events
2) One tour, tasting, and lunch event per year
3) Chet Valley's Guild exclusive harvest supper
4) Blending with the Winemaker

Chet Valley Vineyard is proud to offer wine lovers across the UK the unique opportunity to create and enjoy their own fine English wine using well-established varieties of vines growing on Chet Vineyard through a range of vine rental packages.

The gift of a lifetime, this allows their clients to try their hand at winemaking, getting involved as much, or as little as they desire. With leasing options from 9–50 vines available, Chet Valley leaseholders receive between 15 and 100 bottles of their own wine per year, while benefitting from exclusive vineyard access, an annual complementary tour, invites to leaseholder events, and more.

www.chetvineyard.co.uk
Telephone: 01508 333002
Email: info@chetivneyard.co.uk
Facebook – @chetvalleyvineyard
Twitter – @chetvineyard
Instagram – @chetvineyard

# CHILFORD HALL VINEYARD

## CAMBRIDGESHIRE

CHILFORD HALL, BALSHAM ROAD, LINTON, CAMBRIDGESHIRE, CB21 4LE

- 8 Ha of planted vines

- 18,000 bottles annually

- Winemaker Mark Barnes

- Grape varieties Müller-Thurgau, Schönburger, Ortega, Reichensteiner, Pinot Noir, Rondo, Regent, Dornfelder, Siegerrebe

## TERROIR

Initially planted in 1972, the vineyard is set out over 20 acres of free draining 'flinty' soil which overlays chalk. These soil conditions are similar to those found in the Champagne region of France which makes it ideal for the production of sparkling wines. The vines occupy a south-west facing slope to maximise the sunshine available throughout summer months. The vineyard is situated just 13 km (8 miles) from the historic city of Cambridge amidst tranquil, rolling countryside which is rich in flora and fauna. It is one of England's oldest established vineyards with over 17,000 vines.

## ABOUT

The Chilford Hall estate has been in the Alper family since

1966 when it was bought by the late entrepreneur Sam Alper. Sam Alper had a keen interest in wine, art and sculpture and it is these interests which shapes the development of the estate making it a destination with a profound sense of individuality, wherever you look there is something of beauty and interest for each visitor.

Planting of the first vines took place in 1972, making Chilford Hall vineyard one of the oldest established vineyards in England. Situated amongst the rolling chalk hills of the Cambridgeshire Downs, the estate is a consistent producer of high-quality award-winning wines.

## THE WINE

Since its first planting, the vineyard has grown in size and now covers more than 20 acres, comprised of 9 different vine varieties chosen to perfectly match the climate and soil conditions of the estate. With more than a quarter of a century of expertise, Chilford Hall Vineyard is now a prime visitor attraction, producing more than 18,000 bottles of still and sparkling wine each year.

All of the wines produced on the estate are made exclusively from the grapes grown and harvested here in any given year. This means that each year the wines they produce have a slightly different blend and taste making it a unique drinking experience from one vintage to the next. The estate produces high quality Red, White, Rosé and sparkling wines which have won numerous awards and accolades over recent years.

### Chancellor Sparkling Wine

Made to reflect the softer side of sparkling Brut wine, it is pale straw in colour, effervescent in nature and singing with green apple, pear and lemon zest flavours.

### Graduate Sparkling Wine

Winner of a Bronze Medal at the 2020 IEW (Independent English Wine) Awards and a Bronze Medal at the Decanter World Wine Awards, this sparkling wine is a careful blend of hand selected Müller-Thurgau and Pinot Noir grapes brought together to produce a softer style of Brut Wine.

The wine is clean, fresh and floral with subtle hints of apple and lime.

### Mallyon Sparkling Rosé

Delicate salmon pink in colour, the mousse lifts hints of fresh strawberries before these are joined by citrus overtones. The strawberry, lemon and lime flavours carry on washing the palate through its creamy, mellow finish.

## VISITING AND BUYING

**Buy online at www.chilfordhall.co.uk**
**Email: events@chilfordhall.co.uk**
**Telephone: 01223 895600**

# GIFFORDS HALL VINEYARD

## SUFFOLK

### HARTEST, BURY ST EDMUNDS, SUFFOLK IP29 4EX

- 4.5 Ha of planted vines

- 30,000 bottles annually

- Producer Linda Howard

- Grape varieties Pinot Noir, Pinot Blanc

## TERROIR

Situated on an ancient glacial riverbed, their 19-acre vineyard grows upon fertile sandy loam soil over gravel to produce quality grapes, high in natural sugars and acids, which lend themselves particularly well to sparkling and still wines. It's this special terroir which gives their wines their dry flinty quality and delicate floral accents.

## ABOUT

Since 1986, Giffords Hall Vineyard has been producing exceptional single estate wines from the heart of the Upper Stour Valley, Suffolk. Pinot Blanc, Pinot Noir, both Burgundy clone and Précoce, Madeleine Angevine, Reichensteiner, Rondo and Bacchus varieties thrive here. The vineyard was established with plantings of these modern clones.

Guy and Linda Howard launched the family-run label in 2009, firstly an English sparkling followed by a Rosé, and Bacchus still wine, achieving success at national and international level. Ever proud of their award-winning vineyard, the Giffords Hall brand produces elegant wines of the highest standard. They also have an al fresco cafe.

## THE WINES

### Classic Cuvée

This Classic Cuvée is made using the traditional Champagne method and grapes. Hand-selected Pinot Noir, Burgundy clone, and their favourite Pinot Blanc make up this vintage,

with the base wines barrel fermented in French Limousin oak. It is not, however, a traditional French Champagne. Its structure has the robust acidity and minerality you would expect, but this English cousin has depth, distinctive fruit flavours with a delicate floral twist and a biscuity-dry finish.

### Brut Reserve NV

One of their best-selling sparkling wines, the Brut Reserve NV is a house blend from their barrel-aged reserves. It sits on its lees from a minimum of 11 months before it's bottled, and they wait another year until they deem it right for disgorging. It has a soft fruit character redolent of Red apples and subtle spice.

### Sparkling Suffolk Pink

Traditional-method sparkling Rosé made in their house style. This English sparkling is on the

dry side but balanced by a smooth mouthfeel and length. It has a pale pink rose colour, with a delicate floral nose. A creamy soft mousse, alongside raspberry and redcurrant fruit notes, make up this elegant sparkling wine.

## VISITING AND BUYING

The Cellar Door Shop is open 11 am–4 pm.

In the summer season, you can visit their Stable Door Cafe and sit al fresco in the vines.

Alongside their award-winning wines, their shop sells homewares and local produce.

They also have year-round events, with exhibitions and fairs.

www.giffordshall.co.uk
Telephone: 01284 830799

# Spotlight on
# NEW HALL VINEYARDS

## ESSEX

NEW HALL VINEYARDS, CHELMSFORD ROAD, PURLEIGH, ESSEX CM3 6PN

NEW HALL VINEYARD
- Est 1969 -

- **49 Ha of planted vines**

- **150,000–170,000** bottles for New Hall, of which around a quarter is sparkling wine, plus 30–40,000 bottles for contract winemaking clients

- **Head Winemaker** Stephen Gillham

- **Assistant Winemaker** Tim Underwood

- **Grape varieties** 15 grape varietals, including Bacchus, Pinot noir, Pinot Meunier, Chardonnay, Pinot Gris and the lesser known and grown aromatic varietals including Schonburg, Ortega and Siegerrebe

## TERROIR

New Hall, along with other renowned vineyards in the Crouch Valley, enjoys a unique microclimate aided by a combination of low rainfall, a temperate growing season and ideal growing degree days tempered by the neighbouring River Crouch and Blackwater. The risk of frost is very low and the dry, warm season allows a steady accumulation of flavours to develop in their aromatic varieties. Vines have been planted in Purleigh since the 12th Century which pays testament to the fact that their terroir has been recognised as a successful grape-growing site for centuries.

## THE WINE

In 1983, Piers Greenwood partnered up with Kenneth McAlpine at Lamberhurst Vineyards, Kent, to produce one of the first Traditional Method English Sparkling Wines from Pinot Noir and Chardonnay grapes grown at New Hall.

### New Hall Classic Sparkling Brut

Their 2018 Classic Brut is a classic blend of two noble varieties; Pinot Noir and Chardonnay. Occasionally their Classic Brut is produced with the addition of Pinot Blanc, adding notes of stone fruit and Conference pear. The wine has aromas of ripe apricots, with crisp apple and floral notes on the mid palate.

The clones traditionally grown at New Hall produce fruit-driven, fresh sparkling wines which favour lees ageing of less than 15 months. However, they are looking forward to producing richer, more autolytic sparkling wines in the future with the recent planting of Pinot Meunier.

### New Hall 100% Pinot Noir Sparkling Rosé

Their Sparkling Rosé has proved so popular that they have quadrupled production in the past two years. Produced by whole-bunch pressing Pinot Noir and Chardonnay and selecting the first and best Cuvée for the blend. Their Sparkling Rosé has a delicate mousse, allowing aromas of fresh raspberry and cassis to reach the nose. On the palate, flavours of strawberry and cream come through, leading to an elegant clean finish with some autolytic notes.

### New Hall 2018 Sparkling Bacchus

Produced from the oldest plantation of Bacchus vines in the UK, their Traditional Method Bacchus demonstrates classic hedgerow and elderflower notes on the nose. Flavours of fresh green apple and lemon prevail, with a soft creamy mousse and elegant minerality on the finish.

## VISITING AND BUYING

All wines are available via their online shop. Please contact **newhall@newhallwines.co.uk**.
They also have an on-site Vineyard Shop which is open all year round for discount wine sales and samples. Please check their website **www.newhallwines.co.uk** for details.

# VALLEY FARM VINEYARDS

## SUFFOLK

VALLEY FARM VINEYARDS, RUMBURGH ROAD, WISSETT, SUFFOLK, IP19 0JJ

- 8 Ha **of planted vines**

- **1,500** bottles annually

- Winemaker **Knightor, Tregurthy**

- Vintage information
  **Sundancer 2013**

- Grape varieties **Madeleine Angevine, Auxerrois, Pinot Gris, Pinot Meunier and Pinot Noir**

## TERROIR

Valley Farm Vineyards is an 8 acre site with newly renovated vintage vines. They have 3,000 vines which are now producing fine quality grapes. The Vineyard nestles in an idyllic part of Suffolk, not far from the coast at Southwold in the Waveney Valley. Suffolk is renowned for its local eclectic Food and Drink offering, to which Valley Farm Vineyards' wines make a contribution.

The Vineyards specialise in producing quality grapes for still White and Rosé, sparkling White, and sparkling Blush. The Madeleine Angevine is the grape in the still wine while the Auxerrois, Pinot Gris, Pinot Meunier and Pinot Noir are blended into the sparkling wine. An extra squeeze from the latter gives the blush finish to some vintages.

## ABOUT

Valley Farm Vineyards were established in 1987, expanded in 1992 and sold in 2014 to Elaine Heeler and Vanessa Tucker. In 2021 it was sold to the current owner, Adrian Cox, who is working alongside his son to extend the Vineyard's reach.

Adrian's family have lived in Suffolk for many years. A builder for many years, he decided it was time to turn to something else and went into training to build the vineyard into all it can be. He has big plans for the future and can't wait to make the most out of the beautiful site.

In 2015 the Madeleine Angevine achieved a prestigious UKVA (now WinesGB) Gold Medal, putting it in the top 10%.

## THE WINE

### Madeline Angevine 2018

Award Winning. The summer of 2018 provided them with yet another great single estate vintage. Aromas of stone fruit, walnut, apple and gentle hedgerow flowers are exhibited. The palate is crisp, dry, elegant and very well balanced. Flavours are of citrus and ripe Cox apple.

### English Sparkling Wine 'Sundancer' 2013 Vintage

Bottle fermented in the traditional way and laid down for three years, this is a luscious blend of Pinot Noir, Pinot Meunier and Pinot Gris grapes from Valley Farm Vineyards.

## VISITING AND BUYING

Appointment only.
Email: info@valleyfarmvineyards.co.uk
Telephone: 07867 009967
Website: www.valleyfarmvineyards.co.uk

# WEST STREET VINEYARD

## ESSEX

WEST ST, COGGESHALL, COLCHESTER CO6 1NS

West Street Vineyard

- 1.4 Ha **of planted vines**
- 3,000 **bottles annually**
- **Winemaker** Jane Mohan
- **Grape varieties** Pinot Noir, Chardonnay and German varietal Faber making up the remainder

## TERROIR

On the northern perimeter of the vineyard is the Roman road which connected Colchester to St Albans, at the other, running along the southern end, is the meandering river Blackwater. The river winds its way gently along the valley floor on its way to the sea which it finally reaches at the Heybridge basin a few miles further downstream. Essex is predominantly a rural county of gentle slopes and big skies. What makes it better for vine growing is that it is the driest county in England. West Street sits on a south facing slope at only 30 metres (98 ft) above sea level. Predominantly with Essex clay soils this is interspersed with gravel which helps to keep the vines well drained and flint, which gives their wines their steely minerality and flinty character.

## ABOUT

West Street Vineyard is family-owned at the heart of medieval Coggeshall. The Cistercian order of monks came to the village in 1147, and they believe that they brought wine making with them. With the dissolution of the monastic community in 1538, Thomas Seymour acquired the rich fertile abbey lands and wine making came to a grinding halt for the next 400 years.

However, in 2009, the Mohan family bought an old abandoned site in West Street which had been planted in the early 1980s with 800 Faber vines with a plan to extend the vineyard and plant 3,500 vines with a view to making wine. It was a dream long held – one which had begun in the warm dry southern vineyards of France of the Côtes du Marmandais. During the late 1980s, Jane Mohan went to work in a vineyard one long hot summer between school and university to improve her French. The French did get better, but more importantly perhaps, so too did a lifelong fascination with the vine and how the combination of vine, soil and the vagaries of the weather combine to produce each vintage. Each year the result is different from the last. The dream was turned into a reality some 25 years later and they now make a combination of sparkling White and Rosé wines. The family works the vines themselves, calling upon neighbours in the village and friends at harvest time when everyone shares in a postharvest lunch and a glass of last year's vintage to say thank you for their labour.

## THE WINE

### West Street Sparkling Wine

West Street Sparkling is fruit driven made from almost equal parts of Chardonnay and Pinot Noir. It's a dry sparkling wine with notes of apple, made in the traditional Champagne style. The wine is a delicious combination with the celebrated Colchester natives which have been harvested only a few miles down the road since Roman times.

## VISITING AND BUYING

**Buy online at www.weststreetvineyard.co.uk**
**Email: info@weststreetvineyard.co.uk**
**For opening hours please contact**
**01376 563303**
Enjoy a weekend away only an hour from the City of London in on site vineyard accommodation, coming in 2022.

# WALES AND THE WEST MIDLANDS

Undulating landscapes give rise to some of the oldest and largest vineyards in the country across Wales and the Midlands, with no single distinguishing feature uniting them all. Pinot Noir, a grape variety known for its concentrated base in many sparkling wines, is also grown across this region, owing to the chalky quality of the soil.

Penart.
Cslule

**Kerry Vale Vineyard**

**Halfpenny Green Wine Estate**

**Stonyfield Vineyard**

**Parva Farm Vineyard**

# Spotlight on
# HALFPENNY GREEN WINE ESTATE

## STAFFORDSHIRE

HALFPENNY GREEN WINE ESTATE, TOM LANE, HALFPENNY GREEN, BOBBINGTON, DY7 5EP

- **12 Ha** of planted vines
- **120,000** bottles annually
- **Winemakers** Clive Vickers and Ben Hunt
- **Vintage information** Classic Cuvée 2014, Red Sparkling 2018
- **Grape varieties** Pinot Noir, Chardonnay, Seyval Blanc, Rondo, Regent

## TERROIR

Set in the heart of the Severn Valley, and skirting the Black Country, Halfpenny Green Wine Estate sits within the perfect micro-climate for producing high-quality sparkling wine far outside the traditional heartlands of the English industry. Loamy sand soils atop sandstone creates good water drainage and crisp, aromatic fruit, while the south-west-facing slopes allow for effective frost drainage in the spring, and perfect ripening conditions in the late summer. Vineyard intervention is kept to a minimum, with the upmost respect given to the local environment, and all harvesting is completed by hand with the help of the local community. The sum of all these factors helps to create a wine that gives the truest expression of the landscape of South Staffordshire.

## ABOUT

One of the early pioneers of the modern English wine industry, vines were first planted at Halfpenny Green in 1983 by Martin Vickers on land farmed by his family for three generations previous.

Initially starting with 300 vines as a personal project, Martin soon realised the potential of the site, and by 1991 had expanded the plantings to cover the whole estate.

Nearly 40 years later, Halfpenny Green remains one of the oldest and largest single vineyards in England, covering a total of 12 hectares (30 acres). Martin continues to manage the vineyard, while his son Clive oversees the winery, carrying on the family tradition as the fourth generation to work the estate.

Today, Halfpenny Green maintains its original pioneering spirit, planting England's first

commercial plot of the experimental variety Divico in 2019, winning medals and trophies both nationally and internationally, and remaining at the forefront of the evolution and development of English Sparkling Wine.

## THE WINE

### Brut Sparkling NV

The signature sparkling wine of Halfpenny Green Wine Estate, bringing together a blend of classical English varieties. Pinot Noir brings elegance and character, while Chardonnay adds delicate apple and lemon notes, and Seyval Blanc keeps the blend crisp and exciting. Over 18 months of lees ageing gives complexity and richness, while still allowing the fruit flavour to shine through. A pale gold colour in the glass, with a delicate mousse, and fine, free-flowing bubbles, the Brut typifies English Sparkling Wine from the Midlands.

### Rosé Sparkling NV

A blend of Chardonnay, Pinot Noir, and Seyval Blanc has created this light, crisp, and zippy sparkling Rosé. Pale salmon pink in colour, with fine bubbles, and refined aromas of rose petal and redcurrant. The wine has been aged for over 18 months on its lees to allow complex flavours of raspberry, strawberry, and brioche to develop, and produce an exciting, versatile sparkling Rosé that is just as well suited to serious celebration, as it is to relaxed easy-drinking.

### Classic Cuvée 2014

With 2014 being such a stand-out vintage for Halfpenny Green, this wine was created to take advantage of the perfect conditions. Heavily Pinot

Noir dominated, with a fraction of Chardonnay, the wine has spent over four years ageing on lees, with at least a further year ageing on cork before release. This time and patience has allowed the Classic Cuvée to reach its full potential, creating a sparkling wine that is rich, complex, and characterful, with delicate notes of lemon, green apple, and sweet pastries.

### Red Sparkling 2018

Only produced in the most exceptional years, this out-of-the-ordinary wine showcases the innovation and individualism of both Halfpenny Green and English Sparkling Wine. A blend of Pinot Noir, Seyval Blanc, Rondo, and Regent, this wine has been produced to allow for the maximum extraction of fruit character and colour, while leaving behind the tannins and bitter characters normally associated with Red wines. Lees ageing is kept to a minimum to encourage a fruitier, more delicate style of wine, followed by a minimum of six months ageing in bottle after disgorging before release to ensure the wine reaches its full potential.

VISITING AND BUYING

Open to the public year-round.
www.halfpennygreen.co.uk
Telephone: 01384 221122
Email: info@halfpennygreen.co.uk

# KERRY VALE VINEYARD

## SHROPSHIRE

KERRY VALE VINEYARD, PENTREHEYLING, SHROPSHIRE, SY15 6HU

## TERROIR

Kerry Vale Vineyard is situated on the Shropshire side of the Welsh/English border at the eastern tip of the Vale of Kerry – a rural area of exceptional beauty, just 4.8 km (3 miles) south of the charming town of Montgomery.

Planted in 2010 on stony, free draining soil, the land on which Kerry Vale Vineyard sits is of great archaeological interest. It once formed part of the Roman Fort of Pentreheyling, and is on the edge of a number of Roman marching camps.

As well as their Roman history, two decades of archaeological research show the site was once occupied by Bronze Age funerary monuments, a druid road, and a medieval settlement! With Offa's Dyke just a field away.

## ABOUT

Kerry Vale Vineyard is a family-run business, owned by husband and wife team Russell and Jan Cooke.

In February 2020 they purchased the vineyard from founder Geoff Ferguson. Prior to being a vineyard, the site was home to an old blacksmith's house called Brompton View, sixteen extremely dilapidated buildings and six acres of farm land.

Home to 6,000 vines spaced at 1.2 m (4 ft) in rows 2.3 m (7.5 ft) apart – there are 62 rows with a combined length from the first vine to the last of just under 13 kilometres or approximately 8 miles! The vines are pruned on a Double Guyot trellising system.

## THE WINE

### KVV Sparkling White – Brut (2016/2018)

Made from Kerry Vale's Phoenix grapes, this award winning sparkling English wine is dry and light bodied with a beautiful crisp acidity. Full of toasty notes and fine bubbles. Rounded off with a complex yet delicate finish.

Made using the traditional method it spends a minimum of twenty-four months on lees.

### KVV Sparkling Rosé – Brut (2016/2018)

A delicate blend of Phoenix and Rondo, light in style with soft Red fruits on the palate. Very smooth with fine creamy bubbles and a lovely elegant finish.

Traditional method with a minimum of twenty-four months on lees.

### KVV Sparkling Red – Brut (2018)

Hand crafted in small batches, this is a limited edition release, with only 1,000 bottles produced. Made with 100% Rondo this traditional method sparkling wine has a lovely deep colour with a soft sparkle and dark forest fruit characters.

## VISITING AND BUYING

Kerry Vale Vineyard is open from March to Christmas. Tours are scheduled every Saturday, Sunday and Thursday from April to November. They also take bookings for private tours at other times by special arrangement.

Their café and shop are open from Tuesday to Sunday (closed Mondays).
10am to 4pm – April to October
10am to 3pm – November and December
Telephone: 01588 620627
Email: info@kerryvalevineyard.co.uk
www.kerryvalevineyard.co.uk

# PARVA FARM VINEYARD

## MONMOUTHSHIRE

PARVA FARM VINEYARD, TINTERN, CHEPSTOW, MONMOUTHSHIRE NP16 6SQ

- 1 Ha **of planted vines**
- Approx. 6,000 **bottles per year (1,500 sparkling, 4,500 still)**
- Winemaker **Martin Fowkes of Three Choirs Vineyards, Newent, Glos. GL181LS**
- Vintage information **Most of their wines are vintage but they have occasionally made non-vintage**
- Grape varieties **Seyval Blanc, Huxelrebe, Pinot Noir, Regent**

## TERROIR

Parva Farm Vineyard is situated on a steep, south facing slope overlooking the River Wye and the village of Tintern with its ancient Abbey. The proximity of the river means the site rarely suffers from frost. The trees on the surrounding hills offer shelter from the prevailing south westerly wind. The soil is a light sandy loam over limestone and due to the steep slope is very well drained. The weather is usually mild in winter with little snow and for Wales, not too wet.

## ABOUT

Parva Farm Vineyard was planted in 1979 by the previous owner and was taken over in 1996 by the present owners, Colin and Judith Dudley, when it was in a neglected state. With hard work it was returned to production and the old vines have been producing quality grapes ever since. Working with the winemakers at Three Choirs, many prize-winning wines have been produced over the years. The first wines produced were still wines from the Bacchus grapes and Rosé from the late ripening Pinot Noir grapes. The first sparkling wine was made to be ready for the Millennium celebrations and the first Rosé sparkling to celebrate the Dudleys' ten years at the vineyard. Sparkling wines were initially a special extra but have now become one of the best sellers at the vineyard. Most of the wine is sold from the cellar door.

## THE WINE

### Dathliad Sparkling Brut 2013

This wine was made from Seyval Blanc (80%) and Huxelrebe (20%) which were harvested on 14th October 2013. They were the first grapes harvested that year after a very cold spring caused late flowering. The Seyval Blanc grapes were picked over and only the ripest were harvested leaving the rest for a later pick. The Huxelrebe is fairly early ripening but tends to retain high acidity while also having high sugar levels, making it a good addition to the

Seyval Blanc. This wine was fermented in stainless steel and then bottle fermented for 2 years using Champagne yeast. It was awarded 'Best Welsh Wine' in the English and Welsh Wine of the Year competition in 2016 and a Gold Medal in the Welsh Vineyards annual competition in 2017.

### Dathliad Sparkling Rosé 2013 (Brut)

A combination of Pinot Noir (90%) and Regent (10%) worked really well to produce this lovely Rosé sparkling. The grapes were harvested late due to the late flowering in 2013 with the Pinot noir not being picked until 4th November. However, it was worth the wait as the resulting wine has been one of the most popular they have ever produced. There is plenty of fruit on the palate but fresh crispness too. This wine was on the lees for 3 years. It was awarded medals in both the English and Welsh Wine of the Year competition and the Welsh Vineyards annual competition in 2016. As the vineyard is only small (1 hectare), the sparkling wine production is usually between 500–1000 bottles of any one type making it quite remarkable.

## VISITING AND BUYING

Summer opening hours are 12.00 – 5pm.
The opening hours for their shop during winter are:
Mon:     11.30am – 4pm
Tue:     Closed
Wed:     Closed
Thu:     11.30am – 4pm
Fri:     11.30am – 4pm
Sat:     11.30am – 4pm
Sun:     11.30am – 4pm
Visits outside opening hours can be arranged by contacting them beforehand.
http://www.parvafarm.com/

# PENARTH ESTATE

## POWYS

POOL RD, NEWTOWN SY16 3AN

- **4 Ha** of planted vines
- **12,000** bottles annually
- **Winemakers** Bernard and Tanya Herbert. Martin Fowke
- **Grape varieties** Chardonnay, Pinot Noir and Pinot Meunier

### TERROIR

The vineyard is alongside the River Severn and the slopes face South Westerly.

### ABOUT

Bernard and Tanya Herbert planted their first vines in 1999, and the acreage was increased 2 years later. Varieties that are grown here are the three classical sparkling wine grapes. Penarth Estate sparkling wines have been produced in the traditional method, with two years in stainless steel tanks on lees and a 12-month bottle maturation. The vineyard produces sparkling and still White and Rosé wines as well as brandy and has won medals in the Decanter World Wine Awards and International Wine & Spirits Competition.

## THE WINE

### Penarth Estate Sparkling Wine

The wine has been produced in the traditional method, undergoing second fermentation in the bottle over a long period. The result is a crisp, dry wine with pleasant aromatic flavours to add pleasure to any food.

### Penarth Estate Pink Sparkling Wine

The Penarth Estate Pink Sparkling Wine has been produced in the traditional method, undergoing second fermentation in the bottle over a long period. The result is a fruity wine with harmonious tannins.

## VISITING AND BUYING

**Telephone: 01686 625403**

# STONYFIELD VINEYARD

## NORTHAMPTONSHIRE

30A STOKE ROAD, BLISWORTH, NORTHANTS NN7 3BX

- 0.4 Ha of planted vines

- 500–4,000 bottles annually, (depending on the weather)

- Winemaker Halfpenny Green Wine Estate

- Vintage information Award winning English Sparkling Wine since 2013, including Decanter, WineGB Gold Medal and Trophy winner 2021

- Grape varieties Pinot Noir and Seyval Blanc

## TERROIR

Stonyfield sits on a single one acre field, south facing and sloping down to the Grand Union Canal. In 1793, engineers started work on what was to be the longest tunnel in England and they spread the ironstone rock from the tunnel above the entrance – creating Stonyfield. The result is a well-drained shingle soil, with ironstone spoil sitting above Northamptonshire clay, on which the vines flourish. The top of the field is high, at 116 m (380.5 ft), and is sited well north of most English vineyards. It is very weather dependent, but the unusual terroir produces a wine with a very pleasing character.

## ABOUT

Stonyfield is a very small, family run vineyard, cared for by John Vaughan, his wife Prue and his sister Belinda. Harvests are an informal affair with friends and family pitching in to pick the grapes. The field has been in the family for generations – used in the past to home pigs and then wild flowers. It was planted in 2011 as a memorial for Belinda's husband Mick, who died in 2010 and who had been encouraging the family to plant a vineyard on the site for many years.

John and Belinda both admit it has been a steep but joyful learning curve – made the more enjoyable by winning awards every year since the first harvest in 2013 – with the pinnacle to date in 2021 when Stonyfield Sparkling White 2017 won Gold Medal and the Trophy from WineGB for best sparkling blend. A great way to celebrate their tenth anniversary.

## THE WINE

Stonyfield produces only English Sparkling Wine made by the traditional Champagne Method. Each year, the vineyard aims to produce a Rosé and a White, both using a blend of Pinot Noir and Seyval Blanc grapes. Given the northerly location, the vineyard can be hit by late frosts and harvest size varies considerably year on year. In a harsh year the one acre may produce only 500–600 bottles, but in a good year a bumper harvest can result in over 4,000 bottles. For Stonyfield, the prize is not the quantity but the regular high quality of the grapes.

All wines are allowed over three years to develop before coming to market.

### Sparkling White, 2017

Gold Medal and Dudley Quirk Trophy Winner, 2021, WineGB.
Made from a blend of approximately 20% Pinot and 80% Seyval Blanc. The crispness of the Seyval is softened by the more complex Pinot to produce a sophisticated, dry taste. Oz Clarke and Susie Barrie, WineGB judges, described it as 'bold with bruised red apple fruit and creamy overtures and tangy in the mouth, with spiced nut flavours and plenty of rustic charm'.

### Sparkling Rosé, 2018

Stonyfield Rosé is also a blend of Pinot Noir and Seyval Blanc, but with approximately 70% Pinot Noir. The skins are left in the juice to produce a soft pink hue, ranging from light apricot to warm honey in colour. The result is a dry wine with a hint of Pinot and a pleasing depth of flavour. The 2018 has been left longer on the lees and will be available from early in 2022, benefitting from the additional time spent in the bottle before coming to market.

### Sparkling White, 2018

Made in the same proportions as the 2017, Stonyfield White 2018 is again a dry, crisp White with a pleasant depth of taste and complexity.

## VISITING AND BUYING

The vineyard is open for free tours and samples on the second Sunday of every month. For further details, see website.

Dogs are very welcome. On open days, visitors are welcome to bring their own picnics and relax in the vineyard.

**Buy online at www.stonyfieldwine.co.uk**
**Telephone: 07771 763026**
**Email: info@stonyfieldwine.co.uk**

# NORTH

With its low altitude, warm soils and other benefitting factors, the
North provides an unlikely, but successful climate for the production
of wine. With its often-sloping hills that are touched by sunlight, any
water from rainfall vanishes quickly and with the land facing the sun
the soil is warmed – resulting in the perfect place for a vineyard.

Leventhorpe Vineyard

Renishaw Hall Vineyard

# LEVENTHORPE VINEYARD

## YORKSHIRE

NEWSAM GREEN ROAD, OFF BULLERTHORPE LANE, WOODLESFORD, LEEDS, LS26 8AF

- 2.1 Ha **of planted vines**

- **3 tonnes of grapes per acre per year** some of which is **put by for sparkling wine production**

- **Winemaker George Bowden**

- **Vintage information 2015**

- **Grape varieties Seyval Blanc with a touch of Pinot Noir**

## TERROIR

Leventhorpe realised that site is all-important in England when setting up a vineyard. George had identified the 5-acre site at Leventhorpe when he had driven past the field after a snowy day and noticed how its south-facing slope had caught the sun, allowing the snow to melt before that of fields in the surrounding area. He knew it was an ideal site for wine-growing.

The site is at a low altitude with an average elevation of 24 m (80 feet). It is a south facing slope of light sandy loam topsoil with sand and cracked sandstone underneath, leading down to the Rive Aire, protected by mature trees. It drains extremely quickly and warms up rapidly in spring, giving the vines some protection from the extremes of the weather.

Frost protection in spring is important, as the young shoots on the vine will not tolerate sub-zero temperatures. At Leventhorpe the site rarely suffers from spring frosts after the third week in April due to the topography of the land and its close proximity to a considerably body of water the river, canal and lake.

## ABOUT

They are a long-established vineyard situated in Leeds, founded in 1985, being the first to re-introduce commercial wine growing back into Yorkshire. Leventhorpe is an ideal site for wine growing and one of the very few vineyards that lie within a large city boundary anywhere in the world. From the beginning it has been their aim to produce excellent wines full of character. All of the wines produced at Leventhorpe are made from grapes grown within the five acre vineyard in their purpose built winery. This enables them to control the wine-making process, thus preserving the wines' unique character and identity.

Oz Clarke states that he could recognise Leventhorpe Madeleine Angevine if given a glass anywhere:
"Leventhorpe is a once tasted always remembered kind of wine"
(*BBC Countryfile Magazine*, May 2009)
An excellent warm site, coupled with early ripening varieties has ensured reliable quality over the years.

## THE WINE

### Leventhorpe Yorkshire Brut 2015
This has an apple yeasty, and biscuity nose. The fine mousse and delicate fresh apple flavour develops into a hint of honey with age.

## VISITING AND BUYING

Visitors welcome. Open for sales most days from noon to 3:30pm. If travelling a distance please phone before your journey.
**www.leventhorpevineyard.co.uk**
**Telephone: 0113 288 9088**
**Email: info@leventhorpevineyard.co.uk**

# Spotlight on
# RENISHAW HALL VINEYARD

## DERBYSHIRE

RENISHAW HALL VINEYARD, RENISHAW, DERBYSHIRE, S21 3WB

- **1.5 Ha** of planted vines
- **5,000 bottles** annually
- **Winemaker** Kieron Atkinson
- **Vintage information** Award winning wines from 2011 onwards IWSC, Decanter, WINEGB medalist
- **Grape varieties** Seyval Blanc, Rondo, Madeleine Angevine, Muscat

Image © Jen Miles

## TERROIR

Planted in 1972, Renishaw Hall Vineyard was formerly the most northerly vineyard in the world. Located in a three-sided stone walled pasture that has a radiating effect on the vines, raising the average temperatures by approximately 1 deg C, the land is free draining sandy loam. The majority of the vines are pruned to guyot single and double depending on the strength of growth of the individual vine. The layout of the vineyard is slightly northerly to suit the layout of the land. The vineyard is tended to entirely by hand.

## ABOUT

Ex-army captain Kieron Atkinson shifted his career from leading troops in Afghanistan to winemaking in 2010, and today, produces multiple award-winning wines made from grapes grown at Renishaw Hall Vineyard in north Derbyshire, just 16 km (10 miles) from Sheffield city centre.

After nine fulfilling years in the army and tours of Iraq and Afghanistan, Kieron went back to study, graduating from Plumpton and immediately taking on historic Renishaw Hall Vineyard on the Derbyshire/South Yorkshire border. At a latitude of 53 degrees, 18 minutes north, the vineyard was hailed as the most northerly in the world during the 1980s, and today is one of the oldest in the UK.

Kieron's wines now include Decanter World Wine Award-winners and the grapes grown to produce the still and sparkling wines include Madeline Angevine, Seyval Blanc, Rondo and Muscat.

The wines are produced using grapes grown locally and hand-picked at harvest. In 2018, Kieron even managed to tread a late harvest batch of grapes using the feet of willing volunteers which went on to make the vineyard's first ever Pétillant Naturel known in the industry as 'Pét Nat', a wine which is created using all-natural methods.

## VINEYARD

All of Renishaw's vines are leaf stripped and shoot thinned, giving the fruit maximum exposure to sunlight, increasing lactic acid and decreasing malic acid, resulting in ripe fruit. Leading up to harvest Kieron constantly checks the sugar acid ratio to ensure there is the right balance. Being fairly far north (for grape growing) in the UK, Kieron leaves the fruit on the vine for the longest period possible. During the harvest the fruit is all hand-picked ensuring that no bruised or non-perfect fruit enters the press. The picked fruit is then taken directly to the winery and pressed that day.

## THE WINE

All of the sparkling wines from Renishaw Hall Vineyard are whole bunched press. Following this, the juice is allowed to stand for 24 hours before being racked off. After racking, inoculation takes place with yeast and a MLF bacteria. The yeast is designed to aid the varietal characteristics, while the MLF softens the acids from malic to lactic bacteria. The fermentation is a controlled process and the juice/wine is fermented for approximately three weeks until dry and the sugar has converted to alcohol. Post fermentation, the wine is then racked off its gross lees and allowed to settle for approximately eight weeks. During this period the wine is racked and no fining agents are added as it will become stable during the secondary fermentation process making it a vegan and gluten free product. During March the year after harvest the wines are put through secondary fermentation (traditional method) and bottled. After the bottling the wines are stored in the dark at a constant temperature for at least 18 months. This allows time for the autolytic flavours to develop, without this time the wines would 'just' be fruity. Following the secondary fermentation stage the wines are disgorged and dosage is added to ensure that there is the required sugar to acid ratio.

### Renishaw Hall White Sparkling

Appearance fine small bubbles and light mousse with a light straw hue.
Aroma hints of lemon zest and brioche
Taste firm acidity provides great structure to a young vibrant clean sparkling wine with hints of citrus and freshly baked biscuits.
The 2011 won a Decanter World Wine award.
UKVA Silver, Decanter Bronze.

### Renishaw Hall Rosé Sparkling

Appearance fine bubbles and light mousse with a light salmon pink tone.
Aroma raspberry, wild strawberry and hint of Bakewell Tart.
Taste wild fruit, balanced acidity, with 2 years' secondary fermentation producing autolytic notes. Simply delicious.
MVA Gold, Decanter Commended.
Drinking well now and will improve for a further 10 years.

### VISITING AND BUYING

For all bookings and enquiries visit:
**www.englishwineproject.co.uk/**
**www.renishaw-hall.co.uk/vineyard**

Images: Left and Top Right
© Charlotte Graham
Photography
Bottom Right © Jen Miles

# GLOSSARY
# ENGLISH SPARKLING WINE

**Acidity** This refers to the crispness of a wine. A more acidic wine will taste sour and sharp, and a less acidic wine will taste more flat. Less acidic wines tend to be from cooler climates.

**Appellation** The legally defined area in which the grapes used for the wine were grown. A wine must fulfil specific guidelines to be considered as part of the appellation.

**Aroma** This describes the scent of the wine, unique to the grape variety. For example: fruits, flowers, or oak.

**Attack** The first sensation or taste of the wine in the mouth.

**Austere** An austere wine is quite hard and lacks roundness.

**Blend** A wine that is produced with more than one grape. The main varieties that go into sparkling wine are Chardonnay, Pinot Noir and Pinot Meunier.

**Body** A wine's body is the product of a combination of characteristics that work together to produce a sense of depth and weight to the wine. A wine can be light, medium or full-bodied.

**Bouquet** The collection of aromas a wine has.

**Budburst** This occurs in the spring when the vines start to produce their first shoots for the growing season.

**Buttery** A term to describe a butter-like character of wine, often found in Chardonnay.

**Complexity** This refers to the combination of many odours, flavours and characteristics that contribute to the quality of a wine.

**Concentrated** This denotes that a wine has a certain depth and richness of flavour.

**Crisp** A crisp wine tends to be higher in acidity and fairly dry, with an absence of sugar. This contributes to a fresh sensation, present in many sparkling wines.

**Cuvée** This describes a special blend or bottling of a specific wine, such as the wines produced by the vineyards in this book.

**Delicate** This refers to a light wine, such as sparkling wines.

**Depth** Associated with the complexity of the wine, this refers to the aroma, taste and texture of a grape and wine.

**Dry** A dry wine contains no sugar as all the residual sugar is fermented in the winemaking process.

**Earthy** A positive characteristic, this refers to a wine that doesn't have a fruity taste, but rather has notes similar to mushrooms, forest floor or leaves.

**Elegant** A wine described as elegant is a light wine with refined characteristics and textures.

**Endnote** Also described as the finish of a wine, this is the taste that is left on the palate after the wine is swallowed. Typically, a longer endnote denotes a higher quality of wine.

**Extract** The materials in wine that are not water, sugar, alcohol or acidity. They make up around 1–1.5% of a wine.

**Exuberant** This will refer to a young wine that is fresh and lively.

**Fermentation** This is the process by which sugars are converted into alcohol.

**Fining** This process uses agents such as egg whites or gelatine to clarify the wine by separating sediment.

**Firm** A firm wine will have a higher tannic content and is more structured.

**Floral** The aroma and taste of a floral wine will mimic the perfume of certain flowers, and can be present in both Red and White wine.

**Fruity** A sweet wine that refers to notes of certain fruits, usually peach, mango and pineapple in a White sparkling wine.

**Hard** A hard wine has rough tannins and usually quite a high acidity.

**Honeyed** A characteristic common in sweet White wines, giving a honey-like taste to the wine.

**Lees** This is the by-product of fermentation that sinks to the bottom of wine, which tend to be deposits of yeast cells, seeds, stems and pulp.

**Legs** The droplets that run down the side of the glass after swirling the wine. It is contested whether they actually denote the quality of the wine or not.

**Length** The amount of time the flavour of the wine remains in the mouth after swallowing. If this time is longer, it suggests a higher quality wine.

**Lift** A characteristic of a wine that comes from acidity giving a refreshing sensation. Without lift, a wine would feel much more flat.

**Maceration** A process in winemaking when colour, flavour and tannins are transferred from the grapes, seeds, skin and pulp into the wine.

**Mature** This refers to a wine that has aged to the extent that all of its elements and characteristics combine to their best effects. Wines often mature over periods from months to years.

**Minerality** This is a unique quality to wine that gives an aroma or taste that is different to a fruity or floral flavour. It comes from grapes grown in mineral laden soils and is specific to particular regions.

**Must** This is the unfermented grape juice containing the skins, seeds and stems of the grapes.

**Natural Wine** A wine with no synthetic or artificial ingredients.

**Nose** This describes how a wine smells in the glass.

**Oenology** The study of wine and winemaking.

**Old vines** Older vines tend to produce more concentrated fruit with naturally lower yields.

**Open** This refers to a young wine which displays its flavours and characteristics early.

**Phenolics** Produced from the pulp, skins, seeds and stems of the grapes, these are important compounds in the wine.

**Pressing** The process in winemaking where juice is extracted from the grapes, either with aid of a press or by hand. In White wine production, this takes place after crushing and before primary fermentation.

**Pure** A pure wine allows the expression of the grape to come through and is a valued quality in wine.

**Racking** This is the process in which wine is transferred from one vessel to another in order to remove all sediment.

**Residual sugar** The sugar in a finished wine that wasn't fermented.

**Rich** A rich wine will give a long endnote as well as abundant texture and flavour, with a full body.

**Secondary Fermentation** This is the winemaking process by which still wine is made into sparkling wine.

**Sediment** These are compounds at the bottom of the wine made up of tannins and pigments that emerge from the wine during the ageing process. It is removed before the wine is drunk through decanting.

**Silky** A wine that feels polished in the mouth.

**Smoky** This characteristic occurs in a wine due to either the char in the barrels, the soil or the grapes and contributes significantly to the aroma.

**Smooth** Smooth wines are soft on the palate and tend to have velvety or silky textures.

**Sorting** The last step in the winemaking process before fermentation where all the unripe grapes and unwanted materials are removed.

**Structure** This refers to the balance between the fruit, alcohol, acidity, tannins and other components in the wine.

**Sweet** This refers to the way in which the residual sugars left in the wine after fermentation combine with other characteristics to give the wine a sweet aroma and texture.

**Tannins** These are the compounds in a wine that contribute to a dry feeling in the mouth, adding to the wine's body.

**Terroir** The land on which the grapes are grown. Environmental factors such as soil types, climate and topography combine to create a specific landscape that suits a specific grape.

**Typicity** The degree to which a particular wine tastes similar to other wines in the region where the grape was grown.

**Vintage** A wine in which all the grapes were harvested and made into wine in the same year.

# VINEYARDS DIRECTORY

| VINEYARD NAME | VINEYARD COUNTY | SPARKLING WHITE | SPARKLING ROSÉ | SPARKLING RED |
|---|---|---|---|---|
| Abbey Vineyard Group | Buckinghamshire | ● | ○ | ○ |
| a'Beckett's Vineyard | Wiltshire | ● | ○ | ○ |
| Albourne Estate | West Sussex | ● | ● | ○ |
| Alder Ridge Vineyard | Berkshire | ● | ○ | ○ |
| Aldwick Estate | North Somerset | ● | ○ | ○ |
| Ancre Hill Vineyards | Monmouthshire | ● | ● | ● |
| Artelium Wine Estate | Sussex | ● | ● | ○ |
| Ashling Park Vineyard | West Sussex | ● | ● | ○ |
| Ashling Park Vineyard – Coldharbour Vineyard | West Sussex | ● | ● | ○ |
| Avalon Vineyard | Somerset | ● | ○ | ○ |
| Bardfield Vineyard | Essex | ● | ○ | ○ |
| Barnsole Vineyard | Kent | ● | ○ | ○ |
| Bath Sparkling Wine (Corston Fields) | BANES | ● | ● | ○ |
| Bearley Vineyard | Warwickshire | ● | ○ | ○ |
| Beaulieu Vineyard | Hampshire | ● | ○ | ○ |
| Bee Tree Vineyard | Sussex | ● | ○ | ○ |
| Biddenden Vineyard | Kent | ● | ● | ○ |
| Black Chalk Wine | Hampshire | ● | ● | ○ |
| Black Dog Hill Vineyard | East Sussex | ● | ● | ○ |
| Black Mountain Vineyard | Herefordshire | ● | ● | ○ |
| Blackboys Vineyard (Tickerage Wines) | East Sussex | ● | ● | ○ |
| Blackdown Ridge Estate | West Sussex | ○ | ● | ○ |
| Bluebell Vineyard Estates | East Sussex | ● | ● | ● |
| Bluestone Vineyards | Wiltshire | ● | ● | ○ |
| Bolney Wine Estate – Pookchurch Vineyard | East Sussex | ● | ● | ● |
| Bosue Vineyard | Cornwall | ● | ● | ○ |
| Bothy Vineyard | Oxfordshire | ○ | ● | ○ |
| Bow-in-the-Cloud Vineyard | Wiltshire | ● | ● | ○ |
| Brabourne Vineyard | Kent | ● | ○ | ○ |
| Breaky Bottom Vineyard | East Sussex | ● | ○ | ○ |
| Breezy Ridge Vineyard | Dorset | ● | ○ | ○ |
| Bride Valley Vineyard | Dorset | ● | ● | ○ |
| Bridewell Organic Gardens | Oxfordshire | ● | ○ | ○ |
| Brightwell Vineyard | Oxfordshire | ● | ○ | ○ |
| Brissenden Vineyard | Kent | ● | ○ | ○ |
| Brook Hill Vineyard | Hampshire | ● | ● | ○ |
| Busi-Jacobsohn Wine Estate | East Sussex | ● | ● | ○ |
| Calancombe Vineyard | Devon | ● | ○ | ○ |
| Camel Valley Vineyard | Cornwall | ● | ● | ○ |

| VINEYARD NAME | VINEYARD COUNTY | SPARKLING WHITE | SPARKLING ROSÉ | SPARKLING RED |
|---|---|---|---|---|
| Carden Park Vineyard | Cheshire | ● | ● | ○ |
| Carr Taylor Vineyard | East Sussex | ● | ● | ○ |
| Castle Brook Vineyard | Herefordshire | ● | ● | ○ |
| Castlewood Vineyard | Devon | ● | ● | ○ |
| Chafor Wine Estate | Buckinghamshire | ● | ● | ○ |
| Chapel Down Wines – Court Lodge Vineyard | Kent | ● | ● | ○ |
| Charles Palmer Vineyard | East Sussex | ● | ● | ○ |
| Chartham Vineyard | Kent | ● | ● | ○ |
| Chet and Waveney Valley Vineyard | Norfolk | ● | ● | ○ |
| Chilford Hall Vineyard | Cambridgeshire | ● | ● | ○ |
| Chiltern Valley Vineyard (Old Luxters) | Oxfordshire | ● | ● | ○ |
| Chilworth Manor Vineyard | Surrey | ○ | ● | ○ |
| Chinthurst Hill Vineyard | Surrey | ● | ○ | ○ |
| Clayhill Vineyard | Essex | ● | ● | ○ |
| Coates & Seely | Hampshire | ● | ● | ○ |
| Colehurst Vineyard | Shropshire | ● | ● | ○ |
| Compton Green Vineyard | Gloucestershire | ● | ● | ○ |
| Conwy Vineyard (Gwinllan Conwy) | Conwy | ● | ● | ○ |
| Coolhurst Vineyard | West Sussex | ○ | ● | ○ |
| Coombe Head Meadow Vineyard (Gourmet Leaves) | Devon | ○ | ○ | ○ |
| Court Garden Vineyard | East Sussex | ● | ● | ○ |
| Croffta Vineyard | Vale of Glamorgan | ● | ○ | ○ |
| Crouch Ridge Vineyard | Essex | ● | ○ | ○ |
| Dalwood Vineyard | Devon | ● | ● | ○ |
| Danebury Vineyards | Hampshire | ● | ○ | ○ |
| Davenport Vineyard – Horsmonden | Kent | ● | ● | ○ |
| Daws Hill Vineyard | Buckinghamshire | ● | ● | ○ |
| Dedham Vale Vineyard | Suffolk | ● | ○ | ○ |
| Denbies Wine Estate | Essex | ● | ● | ○ |
| Dinton Vineyard | Buckinghamshire | ● | ○ | ○ |
| Downsview Vineyard | East Sussex | ● | ○ | ● |
| Dunleavy Vineyards | North Somerset | ● | ○ | ● |
| Dunesforde | Yorkshire | ● | ● | ● |
| D'Urberville Wine Estate | Dorset | ● | ● | ○ |
| Easing Hill Vineyard (Chapel House) | Worcestershire | ● | ○ | ○ |
| East Meon Vineyard | Hampshire | ● | ○ | ○ |
| Eglantine Vineyard | Surrey | ● | ● | ○ |
| Elham Valley Vineyard | Nottinghamshire | ● | ○ | ○ |
| English Oak Vineyard | Dorset | ● | ● | ○ |
| English Wine Project (Renishaw Hall Wines) | Derbyshire | ● | ● | ○ |
| Exton Park Vineyard | Hampshire | ● | ● | ○ |

| VINEYARD NAME | VINEYARD COUNTY | SPARKLING WHITE | SPARKLING ROSÉ | SPARKLING RED |
|---|---|:---:|:---:|:---:|
| Fairmile Vineyard | Oxfordshire | ● | ● | ○ |
| Far Acre Farm Vineyard | Kent | ● | ● | ○ |
| Fawley Vineyard | Buckinghamshire | ● | ○ | ○ |
| Fenny Castle Vineyard | Somerset | ● | ● | ○ |
| Fleurfields Vineyard | Northamptonshire | ● | ● | ● |
| Flint Vineyard | Norfolk | ○ | ● | ○ |
| Forty Hall Vineyard | London | ● | ○ | ○ |
| Frome Valley Vineyard | Herefordshire | ● | ○ | ○ |
| Furleigh Estate | Dorset | ● | ● | ○ |
| Furnace Farm Barn | Herefordshire | ● | ● | ○ |
| Giffords Hall Vineyard | Suffolk | ● | ● | ○ |
| Glyndŵr Vineyard | Vale of Glamorgan | ● | ● | ○ |
| Godstone Vineyards | Surrey | ○ | ● | ○ |
| Greyfriars Vineyard | Surrey | ● | ● | ○ |
| Grange Estates Wine | Hampshire | ● | ● | ○ |
| Grove Estate Vineyard | Staffordshire | ● | ● | ● |
| Guilden Gate Vineyard | Hertfordshire | ○ | ○ | ○ |
| Gusbourne Estates | Kent | ● | ● | ○ |
| Hale Valley Vineyard | Buckinghamshire | ● | ○ | ○ |
| Halfpenny Green Vineyard | Staffordshire | ● | ● | ● |
| Hambledon Vineyard | Hampshire | ● | ● | ○ |
| Hanwell Wine Estate | Nottinghamshire | ● | ● | ○ |
| Harrow & Hope Vineyard | Buckinghamshire | ● | ● | ○ |
| Hattingley Valley Vineyard | Hampshire | ● | ● | ○ |
| Hazel End Vineyard – Three Squirrels | Essex | ● | ○ | ○ |
| Hencote Vineyard | Shropshire | ● | ○ | ○ |
| Hendred Vineyard | Oxfordshire | ● | ○ | ○ |
| Henners Vineyard | East Sussex | ● | ● | ○ |
| Hidden Spring Vineyard | East Sussex | ● | ○ | ○ |
| High Clandon Vineyard | Surrey | ● | ○ | ○ |
| Hollow Lane Vineyard | East Sussex | ● | ● | ○ |
| Holy Vale Wines Ltd | Isles of Scilly | ● | ● | ○ |
| Humbleyard Vineyard | Norfolk | ● | ● | ○ |
| Hundred Hills Vineyard | Oxfordshire | ● | ● | ● |
| Hush Heath Estate | Kent | ● | ● | ○ |
| Huxbear Vineyard | Devon | ● | ○ | ○ |
| Jenkyn Place Vineyard | Hampshire | ● | ● | ○ |
| Kents Green Vineyard | Gloucestershire | ● | ○ | ○ |
| Kerry Vale Vineyard | Shropshire | ● | ● | ● |
| Kingfishers' Pool Vineyard | Leicestershire | ● | ● | ○ |
| Knightor Winery – Seaton Vineyard | Cornwall | ● | ● | ○ |

| VINEYARD NAME | VINEYARD COUNTY | SPARKLING WHITE | SPARKLING ROSÉ | SPARKLING RED |
| --- | --- | --- | --- | --- |
| Laithwaites – Windsor Great Park Vineyard | Berkshire | ● | ○ | ○ |
| Lamberhurst Vineyard | Kent | ● | ○ | ○ |
| Langham Wine Estate | Dorset | ● | ● | ○ |
| Lansdowne Vineyard (Albury Vineyard) | Surrey | ● | ● | ○ |
| Lavenham Brook Vineyard | Suffolk | ● | ○ | ○ |
| Leckford Estate Vineyard | Hampshire | ● | ○ | ○ |
| Leventhorpe Vineyard | West Yorkshire | ● | ○ | ○ |
| Lily Farm Vineyard | Devon | ● | ● | ○ |
| Limeburn Hill Vineyard | Bristol | ● | ● | ● |
| Linch Hill Vineyard | Oxfordshire | ● | ● | ○ |
| Little Oak Vineyard | Gloucestershire | ● | ○ | ○ |
| Little Waddon Vineyard | Dorset | ● | ○ | ○ |
| Little Wold Vineyard | East Yorkshire | ● | ● | ○ |
| Llanerch Vineyard | Vale of Glamorgan | ● | ● | ○ |
| Lordship's Farm Vineyard | Hertfordshire | ● | ○ | ○ |
| Lowick Vineyard | Northamptonshire | ● | ○ | ○ |
| Lympstone Manor Vineyard | Devon | ● | ○ | ○ |
| Mannings Heath – Leonardslee Vineyard | East Sussex | ● | ○ | ○ |
| Mannings Heath Vineyard | West Sussex | ● | ○ | ○ |
| Marden Organic Vineyard - Herbert Hall Wines | Kent | ● | ● | ○ |
| Marlings Vineyard | Hampshire | ● | ● | ○ |
| Martin's Lane Vineyard | Essex | ● | ○ | ○ |
| Melbury Vale Vineyard | Dorset | ● | ● | ○ |
| Meopham Valley Vineyard | Kent | ● | ● | ○ |
| Mereworth Wines | Kent | ● | ● | ○ |
| Mount Vineyard, The | Kent | ● | ● | ● |
| Mountfield Vineyard | East Sussex | ● | ● | ○ |
| Mowbarton Estate (Mudgley Farm) | Somerset | ● | ○ | ○ |
| New Hall Vineyards | Essex | ● | ● | ○ |
| New Lodge Vineyard | Northamptonshire | ● | ○ | ○ |
| Nutbourne Vineyards | West Sussex | ● | ● | ○ |
| Nyetimber – Manor Vineyard | West Sussex | ● | ● | ○ |
| Oaken Grove Vineyard | Oxfordshire | ● | ● | ○ |
| Oastbrook Estates | East Sussex | ○ | ● | ○ |
| Oatley Vineyard | Somerset | ● | ○ | ○ |
| Old Hall Farm Vineyard | Norfolk | ● | ○ | ○ |
| Old Walls Vineyard | Devon | ● | ● | ○ |
| Ovens Farm Vineyard | Lincolnshire | ○ | ● | ○ |
| Oxney Organic Estate | East Sussex | ● | ● | ○ |
| Painshill Park Vineyard | Surrey | ○ | ● | ○ |
| Painters Vineyard (Stoneyfield Wine) | Northamptonshire | ● | ● | ○ |

| VINEYARD NAME | VINEYARD COUNTY | SPARKLING WHITE | SPARKLING ROSÉ | SPARKLING RED |
|---|---|---|---|---|
| Pamela Morley (Priors Dean Vineyard) | Hampshire | ● | ○ | ○ |
| Parva Farm Vineyard | Monmouthshire | ● | ● | ○ |
| Pebblebed – Ebford Eden Community Vineyard | Devon | ● | ● | ○ |
| Pen-y-Clawdd Vineyard | Monmouthshire | ○ | ● | ○ |
| Perch Hill Vineyard | Somerset | ● | ○ | ○ |
| Pewley Down Vineyard | Surrey | ● | ● | ○ |
| Plumpton Estate Rock Lodge Vineyard | West Sussex | ● | ● | ○ |
| Polgoon Vineyard | Cornwall | ● | ○ | ○ |
| Poppydown Vineyard & Winery *(Sparkling Elderflower and Sparkling Rhubarb Wines)* | Hampshire | ○ | ● | ○ |
| Poulton Hill Vineyard | Gloucestershire | ● | ● | ○ |
| Poynings Grange Vineyard | West Sussex | ● | ● | ○ |
| Priors Dean Vineyard | Hampshire | ● | ○ | ○ |
| Raimes Family Vineyard | Hampshire | ● | ● | ○ |
| Rathfinny Estate | East Sussex | ● | ● | ○ |
| Redfold Vineyards – Ambriel Sparkling Wine | West Sussex | ● | ● | ○ |
| Renishaw Hall Vineyard | Derbyshire | ● | ○ | ○ |
| Ridgeview Wine Estate | East Sussex | ● | ● | ○ |
| Road Green Vineyard | Gloucestershire | ● | ● | ○ |
| Roebuck Estates | Sussex | ● | ● | ○ |
| Rosemary Vineyard | Isle of Wight | ● | ● | ○ |
| Saffron Grange Vineyard | Essex | ● | ● | ○ |
| Sanden Vineyard | Kent | ● | ● | ○ |
| Sandridge Barton Wines | Devon | ● | ● | ○ |
| Scaddows Vineyard | Derbyshire | ○ | ● | ○ |
| Seer Green Vineyard | Buckinghamshire | ● | ● | ○ |
| Sharpham Vineyard | Devon | ● | ● | ○ |
| Shawsgate Vineyard | Suffolk | ● | ● | ○ |
| Sheffield Park Vineyard | East Sussex | ● | ○ | ○ |
| Shotley Vineyard *(White sparkling wine yet to be released)* | Suffolk | ● | ○ | ○ |
| Sidbury Vineyard | Devon | ● | ● | ○ |
| Simpson's Wine Estate - Dover Road | Kent | ● | ● | ○ |
| Simpson's Wine Estate - South Barham Road | Kent | ● | ● | ○ |
| Sixteen Ridges Vineyard | Worcestershire | ● | ● | ○ |
| Somborne Valley Vineyard | Hampshire | ● | ● | ○ |
| South Pickenham Estate Vineyard | Norfolk | ● | ○ | ○ |
| Southcott Vineyard | Wiltshire | ● | ○ | ○ |
| Spuncombe Bottom Vineyard | Gloucestershire | ● | ○ | ○ |
| Squerryes Estate – Charmans Farm Vineyard | Kent | ● | ● | ○ |
| Squerryes Estate – Gaysham Farm Vineyard | Kent | ● | ● | ○ |
| Stanlake Park Wine Estate | Berkshire | ● | ● | ○ |

| VINEYARD NAME | VINEYARD COUNTY | SPARKLING WHITE | SPARKLING ROSÉ | SPARKLING RED |
|---|---|:---:|:---:|:---:|
| Staverton Vineyard | Suffolk | ● | ○ | ○ |
| Stonyfield Wine | Northamptonshire | ● | ● | ○ |
| Sugarloaf Vineyard | Monmouthshire | ● | ○ | ○ |
| Sugrue South Downs | Sussex | ● | ○ | ○ |
| Summerhouse Vineyard | South Yorkshire | ○ | ● | ○ |
| Sutton Ridge Vineyard | North Somerset | ○ | ● | ○ |
| Swanaford Vineyard | Devon | ● | ● | ○ |
| Terlingham Vineyard | Kent | ● | ● | ○ |
| The Uncommon | South East | ● | ● | ○ |
| Thelnetham Vineyard | Norfolk | ● | ○ | ○ |
| Three Choirs Vineyard | Gloucestershire | ● | ● | ○ |
| Tinwood Estate | West Sussex | ● | ● | ○ |
| Tregoninny Vineyard | Cornwall | ● | ● | ○ |
| Trevibban Mill Vineyard | Cornwall | ● | ● | ○ |
| Trotton Estate Vineyards | West Sussex | ● | ○ | ○ |
| Tuffon Hall Vineyard | Essex | ● | ● | ○ |
| Vagabond Wines | London | ○ | ● | ○ |
| Valley Farm Vineyards | Suffolk | ● | ○ | ○ |
| Velfrey Vineyard | Pembrokeshire | ● | ○ | ○ |
| Vigornia Wine – Walcot Vineyard | Worcestershire | ● | ○ | ○ |
| Vranken-Pommery Monopole (Louis Pommery England) | Hampshire | ● | ○ | ○ |
| Wake Court Vineyard (Sherborne Castle) | Dorset | ● | ● | ○ |
| Walton Brook Vineyard | Leicestershire | ● | ● | ○ |
| Wayford Vineyard | Somerset | ● | ○ | ○ |
| Welcombe Hills Vineyard | Warwickshire | ○ | ○ | ○ |
| Welland Valley Vineyard | Northamptonshire | ● | ● | ○ |
| Wellhayes Vineyard | Devon | ● | ○ | ○ |
| West Street Vineyard | Essex | ● | ● | ○ |
| Westwell Wine Estates | Kent | ● | ○ | ○ |
| Weyborne Estate | West Sussex | ● | ○ | ○ |
| White Castle Vineyard | Monmouthshire | ● | ● | ○ |
| Winbirri Vineyard | Norfolk | ● | ○ | ○ |
| Wiston Estate – North Farm Vineyard | West Sussex | ● | ● | ○ |
| Wolstonbury | Sussex | ● | ● | ○ |
| Woodchester Valley Vineyard | Gloucestershire | ● | ● | ○ |
| Woodchurch Wine Estate | Kent | ● | ● | ○ |
| Woodreed Vineyard | East Sussex | ● | ○ | ○ |
| Woolton Vineyard | Kent | ○ | ● | ○ |
| Wyfold Vineyard | Oxfordshire | ● | ● | ○ |
| Wyken Vineyard | Suffolk | ● | ○ | ○ |
| Yearlstone Vineyard | Devon | ● | ● | ○ |

# IWSC AWARDS

| Nyetimber | Blanc de Blancs Brut 2013 (Magnum) | Wine Gold 2021 (97) | 2013 | White |
|---|---|---|---|---|
| Court Garden | Blanc de Noirs Extra Dry 2014 | Wine Gold 2021 (96) | 2014 | White |
| Court Garden | Ditchling Quartet Brut 2014 | Wine Gold 2021 (96) | 2014 | White |
| English Oak Vineyard | Engelmann Brut 2014 | Wine Gold 2021 (95) | 2014 | White |
| Henners | Brut 2014 | Wine Gold 2021 (95) | 2014 | White |
| Langham Wine Estate | Rosé Brut 2017 | Wine Gold 2021 (95) | 2017 | Rosé |
| Nyetimber | Tillington Single Vineyard Brut 2013 | Wine Gold 2021 (95) | 2013 | White |
| Wiston Estate | Cuvée Brut 2015 | Wine Gold 2021 (95) | 2015 | White |

| Wyfold Vineyard | 50th Anniversary Brut 2014 | Wine Silver 2021 (94) | 2014 | White |
|---|---|---|---|---|
| Furleigh Estate | Classic Cuvée Brut 2013 (Magnum) | Wine Silver 2021 (93) | 2013 | White |
| Gusbourne | Reserve Brut 2016 | Wine Silver 2021 (93) | 2016 | White |
| Tinwood Estate | Blanc de Blanc Brut 2017 | Wine Silver 2021 (93) | 2017 | White |
| Trevibban Mill | Blanc de Blancs Brut Nature 2014 | Wine Silver 2021 (93) | 2014 | White |
| Artelium Wine Estate | Curators Cuvée Brut 2014 | Wine Silver 2021 (92) | 2014 | White |
| Furleigh Estate | Rosé Brut NV | Wine Silver 2021 (92) | Non Vintage | Rosé |
| Greyfriars Vineyard | Blanc de Noirs Extra Brut NV | Wine Silver 2021 (92) | Non Vintage | White |
| Greyfriars Vineyard | Reserve Rosé Brut 2015 | Wine Silver 2021 (92) | 2015 | Rosé |
| Mereworth Wines | White From Black Brut 2018 | Wine Silver 2021 (92) | 2018 | White |
| Woodchester Valley | Reserve Cuveé Brut NV | Wine Silver 2021 (92) | Non Vintage | White |
| Aldi | Premium English Sparkling Brut NV | Wine Silver 2021 (91) | Non Vintage | White |
| Breaky Bottom | Brut 2016 | Wine Silver 2021 (91) | 2016 | White |
| Denbies Wine Estate | Cubitt Blanc de Noirs Brut 2014 | Wine Silver 2021 (91) | 2014 | White |
| E.H.Booths & Co | Brut NV | Wine Silver 2021 (91) | Non Vintage | White |
| Grange Estate Wines | The Grange Classic Brut NV | Wine Silver 2021 (91) | Non Vintage | White |
| Harrow & Hope | Blanc de Noirs Brut 2015 | Wine Silver 2021 (91) | 2015 | White |
| Harrow & Hope | Rosé Brut 2018 | Wine Silver 2021 (91) | 2018 | Rosé |
| Langham Wine Estate | Blanc de Blancs Brut 2017 | Wine Silver 2021 (91) | 2017 | White |
| Nyetimber | Cuvee Chérie Demi-Sec NV | Wine Silver 2021 (91) | Non Vintage | White |
| English Oak Vineyard | Wainscot Brut 2014 | Wine Silver 2021 (90) | 2014 | White |
| Grange Estate Wines | The Grange Pink Extra Brut NV | Wine Silver 2021 (90) | Non Vintage | Rosé |
| Hattingley Valley | Blanc de Blancs Brut 2014 | Wine Silver 2021 (90) | 2014 | White |

| | | | | |
|---|---|---|---|---|
| Henners | Brut NV | Wine Silver 2021 (90) | Non Vintage | White |
| Langham Wine Estate | Pinot Meunier Extra Brut 2018 | Wine Silver 2021 (90) | 2018 | White |

| | | | | |
|---|---|---|---|---|
| Asda | Extra Special Brut 2017 | Wine Bronze 2021 (89) | 2017 | White |
| Redfold Vineyards | Ambriel English Reserve Demi-Sec NV | Wine Bronze 2021 (89) | Non Vintage | White |
| Woodchester Valley | Rosé Brut 2018 | Wine Bronze 2021 (89) | 2018 | Rosé |
| Balfour Winery | Tesco Finest English Sparkling Rosé NV | Wine Bronze 2021 (88) | Non Vintage | Rosé |
| Bride Valley | Cremant Brut NV | Wine Bronze 2021 (88) | Non Vintage | White |
| Gusbourne | Rosé Brut 2016 | Wine Bronze 2021 (88) | 2016 | Rosé |
| Henners | Rosé Brut NV | Wine Bronze 2021 (88) | Non Vintage | Rosé |
| Langham Wine Estate | Corallian Classic Cuvée Extra Brut NV | Wine Bronze 2021 (88) | Non Vintage | White |
| Langham Wine Estate | Culver Classic Cuvée Extra Brut NV | Wine Bronze 2021 (88) | Non Vintage | White |
| Ridgeview | Oak Reserve Brut NV | Wine Bronze 2021 (88) | Non Vintage | White |
| Tinwood Estate | Rosé Brut 2018 | Wine Bronze 2021 (88) | 2018 | Rosé |
| Waitrose & Partners | Leckford Estate Brut 2016 | Wine Bronze 2021 (88) | 2016 | White |
| Balfour Winery | Tesco Finest English Sparkling NV | Wine Bronze 2021 (87) | Non Vintage | White |
| Bride Valley | Blanc De Blancs Brut 2017 | Wine Bronze 2021 (87) | 2017 | White |
| Busi Jacobsohn Wine Est | Rosé Extra Brut 2018 | Wine Bronze 2021 (87) | 2018 | Rosé |
| Camel Valley | Cornwall Reserve Brut 2018 | Wine Bronze 2021 (87) | 2018 | White |
| Halfpenny Green | Brut 2018 | Wine Bronze 2021 (87) | 2018 | White |
| Harrow & Hope | No. 5 Reserve Brut NV | Wine Bronze 2021 (87) | Non Vintage | White |
| High Clandon Est Vineyard | The Euphoria Cuvée Brut 2016 | Wine Bronze 2021 (87) | 2016 | White |
| Pommery | Louis Pommery Brut NV | Wine Bronze 2021 (87) | Non Vintage | White |
| Redfold Vineyards | Ambriel Blanc de Noirs Brut 2015 | Wine Bronze 2021 (87) | 2015 | White |
| Roebuck Estates | Rosé de Noirs Brut 2016 | Wine Bronze 2021 (87) | 2016 | Rosé |
| Wiston Estate | Rosé Brut 2014 | Wine Bronze 2021 (87) | 2014 | Rosé |
| Balfour Winery | Blanc De Noirs Brut 2018 | Wine Bronze 2021 (86) | 2018 | White |
| Balfour Winery | Rosé Brut 2017 | Wine Bronze 2021 (86) | 2017 | Rosé |
| Busi Jacobsohn Wine Est | Cuvée Brut 2018 | Wine Bronze 2021 (86) | 2018 | White |
| Camel Valley | Pinot Noir Rosé Brut 2018 | Wine Bronze 2021 (86) | 2018 | Rosé |
| Denbies Wine Estate | Classic Collection Bacchus Brut NV | Wine Bronze 2021 (86) | Non Vintage | White |
| Denbies Wine Estate | Cubitt Blanc de Blancs Brut 2014 | Wine Bronze 2021 (86) | 2014 | White |
| Fox & Fox Mayfield | Inspiration Blanc de Gris Brut 2014 | Wine Bronze 2021 (86) | 2014 | White |
| Greyfriars Vineyard | Blanc de Blancs Brut 2014 | Wine Bronze 2021 (86) | 2014 | White |

| | | | | |
|---|---|---|---|---|
| Greyfriars Vineyard | Classic Cuvée Brut 2014 | Wine Bronze 2021 (86) | 2014 | White |
| Greyfriars Vineyard | Cuvée Royale Brut 2015 | Wine Bronze 2021 (86) | 2015 | White |
| Gusbourne | Blanc de Blancs Brut 2016 | Wine Bronze 2021 (86) | 2016 | White |
| Harrow & Hope | Blanc de Blancs Brut 2015 | Wine Bronze 2021 (86) | 2015 | White |
| Lyme Bay Winery | Reserve Brut NV | Wine Bronze 2021 (86) | Non Vintage | White |
| Lyme Bay Winery | Rosé Brut NV | Wine Bronze 2021 (86) | Non Vintage | Rosé |
| Ridgeview | Blanc de Noirs Brut 2015 | Wine Bronze 2021 (86) | 2015 | White |
| The Uncommon | Gerald Bubbly Bacchus-Chardonnay Brut 2020 | Wine Bronze 2021 (86) | 2020 | White |
| Wyfold Vineyard | 50th Anniversary Rosé Brut 2015 | Wine Bronze 2021 (86) | 2015 | Rosé |
| Beacon Down Vineyard | Rosé Brut 2018 | Wine Bronze 2021 (85) | 2018 | Rosé |
| Court Garden | Rosé Brut 2015 | Wine Bronze 2021 (85) | 2015 | Rosé |
| Flint Vineyard | Charmat Rosé Brut 2019 | Wine Bronze 2021 (85) | 2019 | Rosé |
| Redfold Vineyards | Ambriel Rosé Brut 2015 | Wine Bronze 2021 (85) | 2015 | Rosé |

| | | | | |
|---|---|---|---|---|
| Black Chalk | Classic Brut 2016 | Wine Gold 2020 (95) | 2016 | White |
| Kingscote | Blanc de Noirs Brut 2013 | Wine Gold 2020 (97) | 2013 | White |
| Langham | Blanc de Blancs Brut 2015 | Wine Gold 2020 (96) | 2015 | White |
| Breaky Bottom | Cuvée David Pearson Chardonnay Pinot Brut 2015 | Wine Gold 2020 (95) | 2015 | White |
| Gusbourne | Blanc de Blancs Brut 2015 | Wine Gold 2020 (95) | 2015 | White |
| Ridgeview | Blanc de Blancs Brut 2015 | Wine Gold 2020 (95) | 2015 | White |

| | | | | |
|---|---|---|---|---|
| Camel Valley | Pinot Noir Brut Rosé 2018 | Wine Silver 2020 (94) | 2018 | Rosé |
| Redfold Vineyards | Ambriel Classic Cuvée Brut NV | Wine Silver 2020 (94) | Non Vintage | White |
| Fitz | Brut NV | Wine Silver 2020 (93) | Non Vintage | White |
| Greyfriars Vineyard | Cuvée Royale Brut 2015 | Wine Silver 2020 (93) | 2015 | White |
| Gusbourne | Late Disgorged Reserve Brut 2010 | Wine Silver 2020 (93) | 2010 | White |
| Ridgeview | Fitzrovia Rosé Brut NV | Wine Silver 2020 (93) | Non Vintage | Rosé |
| Fox & Fox | Essence Brut 2015 | Wine Silver 2020 (92) | 2015 | White |
| Harrow & Hope | Brut Reserve NV | Wine Silver 2020 (92) | Non Vintage | White |
| Langham | Culver Classic Cuvée Extra Brut NV | Wine Silver 2020 (92) | Non Vintage | White |
| Louis Pommery | England Brut NV | Wine Silver 2020 (92) | Non Vintage | White |
| Marlings Vineyard | Rosé Brut NV | Wine Silver 2020 (92) | Non Vintage | Rosé |
| Court Garden | Blanc de Blancs Brut 2015 | Wine Silver 2020 (91) | 2015 | White |

| | | | | |
|---|---|---|---|---|
| Gusbourne | Blanc de Noirs 2016 | Wine Silver 2020 (91) | 2016 | White |
| Jenkyn Place | Blanc de Blancs Brut 2015 | Wine Silver 2020 (91) | 2015 | White |
| Langham | Corallian Classic Cuvée Extra Brut NV | Wine Silver 2020 (91) | Non Vintage | White |
| Asda | Asda Extra Special English Sparkling Brut 2015 | Wine Silver 2020 (90) | 2015 | White |
| Beacon Down Vineyard | Blanc de Noirs 2017 | Wine Silver 2020 (90) | 2017 | White |
| Langham | Pinot Meunier Extra Brut 2017 | Wine Silver 2020 (90) | 2017 | White |
| Langham | Rosé Brut NV | Wine Silver 2020 (90) | Non Vintage | Rosé |
| Redfold Vineyards | Ambriel Brut Rosé 2014 | Wine Silver 2020 (90) | 2014 | Rosé |
| Valley Farm Vineyards | Sundancer Brut 2015 | Wine Silver 2020 (90) | 2015 | White |
| Wiston Estate | Blanc de Blancs Brut 2015 | Wine Silver 2020 (90) | 2015 | White |
| Wyfold Vineyard | 50th Anniversary Brut 2014 | Wine Silver 2020 (90) | 2014 | White |

| | | | | |
|---|---|---|---|---|
| Bluebell Vineyard Estates | Hindleap Classic Cuvée Brut 2015 | Wine Bronze 2020 (89) | 2015 | White |
| Bride Valley | Blanc de Blancs Brut 2016 | Wine Bronze 2020 (89) | 2016 | White |
| Gusbourne | Reserve Brut 2016 | Wine Bronze 2020 (89) | 2016 | White |
| Tesco Finest | Finest* in Partnership with Hush Heath Estate Rosé Brut NV | Wine Bronze 2020 (89) | Non Vintage | Rosé |
| Breaky Bottom | Cuvée Michelle Moreau Chardonnay Pinot Brut 2014 | Wine Bronze 2020 (88) | 2014 | White |
| Court Garden | Classic Cuvée Brut 2015 | Wine Bronze 2020 (88) | 2015 | White |
| Direct Wines Production | Windsor Great Park Vineyard Brut 2015 | Wine Bronze 2020 (88) | 2015 | White |
| Greyfriars Vineyard | Blanc De Blancs Brut 2014 | Wine Bronze 2020 (88) | 2014 | White |
| Gusbourne | Rosé 2016 | Wine Bronze 2020 (88) | 2016 | Rosé |
| Hoffmann & Rathbone | Blanc de Blancs Brut 2012 | Wine Bronze 2020 (88) | 2012 | White |
| Jenkyn Place | Classic Cuvée Brut 2014 | Wine Bronze 2020 (88) | 2014 | White |
| Roebuck Estates | Blanc de Noirs Brut 2015 | Wine Bronze 2020 (88) | 2015 | White |
| Tesco Finest | Finest* in Partnership with Hush Heath Estate Brut NV | Wine Bronze 2020 (88) | Non Vintage | White |
| Waitrose & Partners | Leckford Estate Brut 2015 | Wine Bronze 2020 (88) | 2015 | White |
| Woodchester Valley | Rosé Brut 2017 | Wine Bronze 2020 (88) | 2017 | Rosé |
| Balfour Hush Heath Estate | Blanc de Blancs Brut 2014 | Wine Bronze 2020 (87) | 2014 | White |
| Breaky Bottom | Cuvée Jack Pike Seyval Blanc Brut 2015 | Wine Bronze 2020 (87) | 2015 | White |
| Fox & Fox | CV Brut 2014 | Wine Bronze 2020 (87) | 2014 | White |
| Fox & Fox | Mosaic Brut 2015 | Wine Bronze 2020 (87) | 2015 | White |
| Greyfriars Vineyard | Blanc de Noirs Brut NV | Wine Bronze 2020 (87) | Non Vintage | White |
| Greyfriars Vineyard | Classic Cuvée Brut 2014 | Wine Bronze 2020 (87) | 2014 | White |
| Gusbourne | Reserve Brut 2015 | Wine Bronze 2020 (87) | 2015 | White |

| | | | | |
|---|---|---|---|---|
| Harrow & Hope | Blanc De Noirs Brut 2015 | Wine Bronze 2020 (87) | 2015 | White |
| Hattingley Valley | Classic Reserve Brut NV | Wine Bronze 2020 (87) | Non Vintage | White |
| Balfour Hush Heath Estate | Rosé Brut 2016 | Wine Bronze 2020 (86) | 2016 | Rosé |
| Bolney Wine Estate | Blanc de Blancs Brut 2016 | Wine Bronze 2020 (86) | 2016 | White |
| Furleigh Estate | Prestige Cuvée Extra Brut 2014 | Wine Bronze 2020 (86) | 2014 | White |
| Harrow & Hope | Rosé Brut 2017 | Wine Bronze 2020 (86) | 2017 | Rosé |
| Hoffmann & Rathbone | Classic Cuvée Brut 2014 | Wine Bronze 2020 (86) | 2014 | White |
| Lyme Bay Winery | Rosé Brut NV | Wine Bronze 2020 (86) | Non Vintage | Rosé |
| Nutbourne Vineyards | Nutty Brut 2016 | Wine Bronze 2020 (86) | 2016 | White |
| Woodchurch | Blanc de Blancs Brut 2015 | Wine Bronze 2020 (86) | 2015 | White |
| Wyfold Vineyard | 50th Anniversary Rosé Brut 2015 | Wine Bronze 2020 (86) | 2015 | Rosé |
| Bride Valley | Crémant Brut NV | Wine Bronze 2020 (85) | Non Vintage | White |

| | | | | |
|---|---|---|---|---|
| Coates & Seely | Coates & Seely Blanc de Blancs La Perfide 2009 | Gold 2019 (97), Bottle Fermented Sparkling Wine Trophy 2019 | 2009 | White |
| Bride Valley Vineyard Ltd | Bride Valley Rosé Bella 2014 | Gold 2019 (95) | 2014 | Rosé |
| Denbies Wine Estate Ltd | Denbies Greenfields NV | Gold 2019 (95) | Non Vintage | White |
| Harrow & Hope | Harrow & Hope Brut Reserve NV | Gold 2019 (95) | Non Vintage | White |

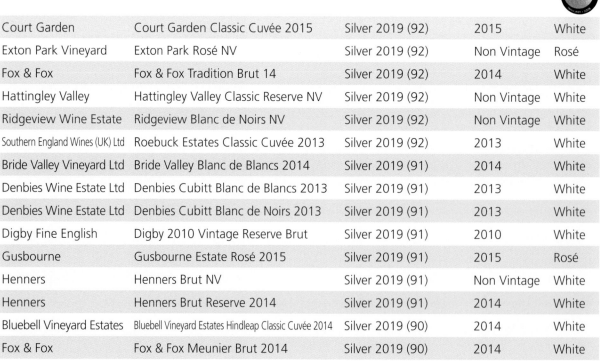

| | | | | |
|---|---|---|---|---|
| Court Garden | Court Garden Classic Cuvée 2015 | Silver 2019 (92) | 2015 | White |
| Exton Park Vineyard | Exton Park Rosé NV | Silver 2019 (92) | Non Vintage | Rosé |
| Fox & Fox | Fox & Fox Tradition Brut 14 | Silver 2019 (92) | 2014 | White |
| Hattingley Valley | Hattingley Valley Classic Reserve NV | Silver 2019 (92) | Non Vintage | White |
| Ridgeview Wine Estate | Ridgeview Blanc de Noirs NV | Silver 2019 (92) | Non Vintage | White |
| Southern England Wines (UK) Ltd | Roebuck Estates Classic Cuvée 2013 | Silver 2019 (92) | 2013 | White |
| Bride Valley Vineyard Ltd | Bride Valley Blanc de Blancs 2014 | Silver 2019 (91) | 2014 | White |
| Denbies Wine Estate Ltd | Denbies Cubitt Blanc de Blancs 2013 | Silver 2019 (91) | 2013 | White |
| Denbies Wine Estate Ltd | Denbies Cubitt Blanc de Noirs 2013 | Silver 2019 (91) | 2013 | White |
| Digby Fine English | Digby 2010 Vintage Reserve Brut | Silver 2019 (91) | 2010 | White |
| Gusbourne | Gusbourne Estate Rosé 2015 | Silver 2019 (91) | 2015 | Rosé |
| Henners | Henners Brut NV | Silver 2019 (91) | Non Vintage | White |
| Henners | Henners Brut Reserve 2014 | Silver 2019 (91) | 2014 | White |
| Bluebell Vineyard Estates | Bluebell Vineyard Estates Hindleap Classic Cuvée 2014 | Silver 2019 (90) | 2014 | White |
| Fox & Fox | Fox & Fox Meunier Brut 2014 | Silver 2019 (90) | 2014 | White |

| Gusbourne | Gusbourne Estate Blanc de Blancs 2014 | Silver 2019 (90) | 2014 | White |
|---|---|---|---|---|
| Harrow & Hope | Harrow & Hope Blanc de Blancs 2014 | Silver 2019 (90) | 2014 | White |
| Langham Wine Estate | Langham Wine Estates Blanc de Blancs 2011 Magnum | Silver 2019 (90) | 2011 | White |
| Langham Wine Estate | Langham Wine Estates Blanc de Blancs Reserve NV | Silver 2019 (90) | Non Vintage | White |
| Ridgeview Wine Estate | Ridgeview Bloomsbury NV | Silver 2019 (90) | Non Vintage | White |
| Waitrose & Partners | Waitrose Leckford Estate Brut 2014 | Silver 2019 (90) | 2014 | White |

| Bolney Wine Estate | Bolney Blanc de Blancs 2016 | Bronze 2019 (89) | 2016 | White |
|---|---|---|---|---|
| Chapel Down | Chapel Down Three Graces 2015 | Bronze 2019 (89) | 2015 | White |
| Court Garden | Court Garden Ditchling Reserve 2014 | Bronze 2019 (89) | 2014 | White |
| Court Garden | Court Garden Rosé 2014 | Bronze 2019 (89) | 2014 | Rosé |
| Digby Fine English | Digby Brut NV | Bronze 2019 (89) | Non Vintage | White |
| Exton Park Vineyard | Exton Park Brut Reserve NV | Bronze 2019 (89) | Non Vintage | White |
| Greyfriars Vineyard | Greyfriars Vineyard Sparkling Rosé Reserve 2014 | Bronze 2019 (89) | 2014 | Rosé |
| Gusbourne | Gusbourne Estate Blanc de Blancs 2013 | Bronze 2019 (89) | 2013 | White |
| Lyme Bay Winery | Lyme Bay Sparkling Rosé NV | Bronze 2019 (89) | Non Vintage | Rosé |
| Upperton Vineyards | Upperton Vineyards Alia 2014 | Bronze 2019 (89) | 2014 | White |
| Woodchester Valley | Woodchester Valley Sparkling Rosé 2016 | Bronze 2019 (89) | 2016 | Rosé |
| Camel Valley | 2016 Camel Valley Pinot Noir Rosé Brut | Bronze 2019 (88) | 2016 | Rosé |
| Chapel Down | Kit's Coty Blanc De Blancs 2014 | Bronze 2019 (88) | 2014 | White |
| Fox & Fox | Fox & Fox Essence Pure Chardonnay Brut 2014 | Bronze 2019 (88) | 2014 | White |
| Furleigh Estate | Furleigh Estate Rosé NV | Bronze 2019 (88) | Non Vintage | Rosé |
| Gusbourne | Gusbourne Estate Brut Reserve 2014 | Bronze 2019 (88) | 2014 | White |
| Hattingley Valley | Hattingley Valley Rosé 2014 | Bronze 2019 (88) | 2014 | Rosé |
| Jenkyn Place | Jenkyn Place Rosé 2014 | Bronze 2019 (88) | 2014 | Rosé |
| Langham Wine Estate | Langham Wine Estates Rosé NV | Bronze 2019 (88) | Non Vintage | Rosé |
| Lyme Bay Winery | Lyme Bay Classic Cuvée 2015 | Bronze 2019 (88) | 2015 | White |
| Bluebell Vineyard Estates | Bluebell Vineyard Hindleap Barrel Aged Blanc de Blancs 2014 | Bronze 2019 (87) | 2014 | White |
| Chapel Down | Chapel Down Classic Non-Vintage Brut NV | Bronze 2019 (87) | Non Vintage | White |
| Chapel Down | Chapel Down Rosé Brut NV | Bronze 2019 (87) | Non Vintage | Rosé |
| Nutbourne Vineyards | Nutty Brut 2015 | Bronze 2019 (87) | 2015 | White |
| Bluebell Vineyard Estates | Bluebell Vineyard Hindleap Blanc de Blancs 2013 | Bronze 2019 (86) | 2013 | White |
| Breaky Bottom | Breaky Bottom - Seyval Blanc 2014 - Cuvée Peter Christiansen | Bronze 2019 (86) | 2014 | White |
| Digby Fine English | Leander Pink Brut NV | Bronze 2019 (86) | Non Vintage | Rosé |

| | | | | |
|---|---|---|---|---|
| Furleigh Estate | Furleigh Estate Classic Cuvée 2014 | Bronze 2019 (86) | 2014 | White |
| Greyfriars Vineyard | Greyfriars Vineyard Classic Cuvée 2013 | Bronze 2019 (86) | 2013 | White |
| Harrow & Hope | Harrow & Hope Brut Rosé 2015 | Bronze 2019 (86) | 2015 | Rosé |
| Vranken Pommery UK Limited | Louis Pommery England NV | Bronze 2019 (86) | Non Vintage | White |
| Wyfold Vineyard | Wyfold Brut 2014 | Bronze 2019 (86) | 2014 | White |
| Denbies Wine Estate Ltd | Chalk Valley English Sparkling Brut NV | Bronze 2019 (85) | Non Vintage | White |
| Langham Wine Estate | Langham Wine Estates Classic Cuvée NV | Bronze 2019 (85) | Non Vintage | White |
| Woodchurch | Woodchurch Rosé 2015 | Bronze 2019 (85) | 2015 | Rosé |

| | | | | |
|---|---|---|---|---|
| Marks and Spencer | Marksman English Sparkling Brut Blanc de Blancs 2014 | Gold 2018, English Sparkling Wine Trophy 2018 | 2014 | White |
| Bluebell Vineyard Estates | Bluebell Vineyard Hindleap Late Disgorged Blanc de Blancs 2008 | Gold Outstanding 2018 | 2008 | White |
| Chapel Down | Kit's Coty Coeur de Cuvée 2013 | Gold Outstanding 2018 | 2013 | White |
| Greyfriars Vineyard | Greyfriars Vineyard Blanc de Blancs 2013 | Gold Outstanding 2018 | 2013 | White |
| Wiston Estate | Wiston Estate Cuvée 2009 | Gold Outstanding 2018 | 2009 | White |
| Breaky Bottom | Breaky Bottom Cuvée Reynolds Stone 2010 | Gold 2018 | 2010 | White |
| Chapel Down | Kit's Coty Blanc de Blancs 2013 | Gold 2018 | 2013 | White |
| Fox & Fox Mayfield | Fox & Fox Meunier Brut 2014 | Gold 2018 | 2014 | White |
| Greyfriars Vineyard | Greyfriars Vineyard Sparkling Rosé Reserve 2014 | Gold 2018 | 2014 | Rosé |

| | | | | |
|---|---|---|---|---|
| Bolney Wine Estate | Bolney Blanc de Blanc 2015 | Silver Outstanding 2018 | 2015 | White |
| Court Garden | Court Garden Blanc de Blancs 2014 | Silver Outstanding 2018 | 2014 | White |
| Hattingley Valley | Hattingley Valley Classic Reserve NV | Silver Outstanding 2018 | Non Vintage | White |
| Ridgeview Wine Estate | Ridgeview Bloomsbury NV | Silver Outstanding 2018 | Non Vintage | White |
| Wyfold Vineyard | Wyfold Brut 2013 | Silver Outstanding 2018 | 2013 | White |
| Blackdown Ridge Estate | Blackdown Ridge Sparkling Vintage 2015 | Wine Artwork & Bottle Design Silver 2018 | 2015 | Rosé |
| Albourne Winery Ltd | Albourne Estate Blanc de Noirs 2013 | Silver 2018 | 2013 | White |
| Albourne Winery Ltd | Albourne Estate Premier Cuvée 2013 | Silver 2018 | 2013 | White |
| Bluebell Vineyard Estates | Bluebell Vineyard Estates Hindleap Rosé 2014 | Silver 2018 | 2014 | Rosé |
| Bluebell Vineyard Estates | Bluebell Vineyard Hindleap Blanc de Blancs 2014 | Silver 2018 | 2014 | White |
| Breaky Bottom | Breaky Bottom Cuvée Cornelis Hendrinkson 2013 | Silver 2018 | 2013 | White |
| Chapel Down | Three Graces 2013 | Silver 2018 | 2013 | White |
| Coates and Seely | Blanc de Blancs La Perfide 2009 | Silver 2018 | 2009 | White |
| Coates and Seely | Rosé La Perfide 2009 | Silver 2018 | 2009 | Rosé |

| | | | | |
|---|---|---|---|---|
| Cottonworth LLP | Cottonworth Classic Cuvée NV | Silver 2018 | Non Vintage | White |
| Court Garden | Court Garden Classic Cuvée 2014 | Silver 2018 | 2014 | White |
| Court Garden | Court Garden Ditchling Reserve 2014 | Silver 2018 | 2014 | White |
| Denbies Wine Estate Ltd | Denbies Cubitt Blanc de Blancs 2013 | Silver 2018 | 2013 | White |
| Denbies Wine Estate Ltd | Denbies Greenfields NV | Silver 2018 | Non Vintage | White |
| Exton Park Vineyard | Exton Park Blanc de Noirs 2013 | Silver 2018 | 2013 | White |
| Fox & Fox Mayfield | Essence Pure Chardonnay Brut 2014 | Silver 2018 | 2014 | White |
| Fox & Fox Mayfield | Lakestreet Vineyard Tradition Blanc de Noir 2014 | Silver 2018 | 2014 | White |
| Greyfriars Vineyard | Greyfriars Vineyard Cuvée NV | Silver 2018 | Non Vintage | White |
| Gusbourne | Gusbourne Estate Blanc de Blancs 2013 | Silver 2018 | 2013 | White |
| Gusbourne | Gusbourne Estate Brut Reserve 2013 | Silver 2018 | 2013 | White |
| Gusbourne | Gusbourne Estate Rosé 2014 | Silver 2018 | 2014 | Rosé |
| Harrow & Hope | Harrow & Hope Brut Reserve NV | Silver 2018 | Non Vintage | White |
| Harrow & Hope | Harrow & Hope Brut Rosé NV | Silver 2018 | Non Vintage | Rosé |
| Haygrove Evolution Ltd | Sixteen Ridges Signature Cuvée 2013 | Silver 2018 | 2013 | White |
| Nutbourne Vineyards | Nutty Brut 2014 | Silver 2018 | 2014 | White |
| Woodchurch | Woodchurch Blanc de Blancs 2014 | Silver 2018 | 2014 | White |
| Woodchurch | Woodchurch Classic Cuvée 2014 | Silver 2018 | 2014 | White |
| Wyfold Vineyard | Wyfold Brut Rosé 2014 | Silver 2018 | 2014 | Rosé |

| | | | | |
|---|---|---|---|---|
| Bluebell Vineyard Estates | Bluebell Vineyard Estates Hindleap Classic Cuvée 2014 | Bronze 2018 | 2014 | White |
| Chapel Down | Chapel Down Classic Non-Vintage Brut NV | Bronze 2018 | Non Vintage | White |
| Coates and Seely | Brut Reserve La Perfide 2011 Magnum | Bronze 2018 | 2011 | White |
| Denbies Wine Estate Ltd | Denbies Cubitt Blanc de Noirs 2013 | Bronze 2018 | 2013 | White |
| Exton Park Vineyard | Exton Park Brut NV | Bronze 2018 | Non Vintage | White |
| Fox & Fox Mayfield | Inspiration Blanc de Gris Brut 2014 | Bronze 2018 | 2014 | White |
| Greyfriars Vineyard | Greyfriars Vineyard Classic Cuvée 2013 | Bronze 2018 | 2013 | White |
| Harrow & Hope | Harrow & Hope Blanc de Noir 2013 | Bronze 2018 | 2013 | White |
| Jenkyn Place | Jenkyn Place Brut Cuvée 2013 | Bronze 2018 | 2013 | White |
| Kingscote Estate & Vineyard Limited | Kingscote Blanc de Blanc NV | Bronze 2018 | Non Vintage | White |
| Kingscote Estate & Vineyard Limited | Kingscote Blanc de Noir NV | Bronze 2018 | Non Vintage | White |
| Ridgeview Wine Estate | Ridgeview Fitzrovia NV | Bronze 2018 | Non Vintage | Rosé |
| Westwell Wine Estates | Westwell Sparkling NV | Bronze 2018 | Non Vintage | White |

# WINE GB AWARDS

| | | | | |
|---|---|---|---|---|
| Wiston Estate Winery | Blanc de Blancs | Top Sparkling Wine | 2015 | White |
| Wiston Estate Winery | Blanc de Blancs | Supreme Champion | 2015 | White |
| Gusbourne | Winery of the year Estate 2021 | | | |
| Wiston Estate Winery | Winery of the year Contract 2021 | | | |
| Ashling Park Estate | Ashling Park Cuvée NV | Best Classic Cuvée NV | NV | White |
| Chapel Down | Kit's Coty Coeur de Cuvée 2015 | Best Prestige Cuvée | 2015 | White |
| Digby Fine English | 2014 Vintage Rosé Brut | Best Sparkling Rosé | 2014 | Rosé |
| Greyfriars Vineyard | Cuvée Royale 2015 | Best Classic Cuvée Vintage | 2015 | White |
| Harrow & Hope | Blanc de Noirs 2015 | Best Blanc de Noirs | 2015 | White |
| Painters Vineyard | Stonyfield Sparkling White 2017 | Best Sparkling Blend | 2017 | White |
| Wiston Estate Winery | Blanc de Blancs 2015 | Best Blanc de Blancs | 2015 | White |
| Sugrue South Downs | Cuvée Boz 2015 | Boutique | 2015 | White |

| | | | | |
|---|---|---|---|---|
| Chapel Down | Kit's Coty Blanc de Blancs 2015 | Gold | 2015 | White |
| Davenport Vineyards | Limney Estate 2015 | Gold | 2015 | White |
| Denbies Wine Estate | Denbies Blanc de Noirs 2014 | Gold | 2014 | White |
| Digby Fine English | 2013 Vintage Reserve Brut | Gold | 2013 | White |
| Digby Fine English | Non Vintage Brut | Gold | NV | White |
| Exton Park Vineyard | RB32 Brut NV | Gold | NV | White |
| Grange Estate Wines LLP | The Grange CLASSIC NV | Gold | NV | White |
| Gusbourne | Blanc de Blancs 2016 | Gold | 2016 | White |
| Gusbourne | Natural Brut 2014 | Gold | 2014 | White |
| Gusbourne | Nest Selection 2014 | Gold | 2014 | White |
| Halfpenny Green Wine Estate | Rosé Sparkling 2019 | Gold | 2019 | Rosé |
| Harrow & Hope | Brut Rosé 2018 | Gold | 2018 | Rosé |
| Langham Wine Estate | Culver Classic Cuvée NV | Gold | NV | White |
| Langham Wine Estate | Rosé 2017 | Gold | 2017 | Rosé |
| Sugrue South Downs | The Trouble With Dreams 2015 | Gold | 2015 | White |
| Tinwood Estate | Blanc de Blancs 2017 | Gold | 2017 | White |
| Woolton Vineyard | Cuvée No1 2015 | Gold | 2015 | White |

| Alder Ridge Vineyard | Special Cuvée NV | Silver | NV | White |
| Aldwick Estate Ltd | Aldwick Jubilate Classic Cuvée 2017 | Silver | 2017 | White |
| Artelium Wine Estate | Curators Cuvée 2014 | Silver | 2014 | White |
| Artelium Wine Estate | Makers Rosé 2015 | Silver | 2015 | Rosé |
| Black Chalk Wine | Classic 2017 | Silver | 2017 | White |
| Black Chalk Wine | Wild Rosé 2018 | Silver | 2018 | Rosé |
| Blackbook Winery | GMF 2018 | Silver | 2018 | White |
| Bluebell Vineyard Estates | Hindleap Barrel Aged Blanc de Blancs 2016 | Silver | 2016 | White |
| Bluebell Vineyard Estates | Hindleap Ruby 2018 | Silver | 2018 | Red |
| Bolney Wine Estate | Cuvée Rosé 2018 | Silver | 2018 | Rosé |
| Bride Valley Vineyard Ltd | Blanc de Blancs 2017 | Silver | 2017 | White |
| Bride Valley Vineyard Ltd | Dorset Cremant NV | Silver | NV | White |
| Busi Jacobsohn Wine Estate | Busi Jacobsohn Rosé 2018 | Silver | 2018 | Rosé |
| Camel Valley Vineyard | Camel Valley Pinot Noir Rosé Brut 2018 | Silver | 2018 | Rosé |
| Chapel Down | Bacchus 'with a touch of sparkle' 2020 | Silver | 2020 | White |
| Chapel Down | Brut NV | Silver | NV | White |
| Chartham Vineyard | Blanc de Blancs 2018 | Silver | 2018 | White |
| Digby Fine English | Leander Pink Non Vintage | Silver | NV | Rosé |
| East Meon Vineyard | East Meon Berrygarden 2015 | Silver | 2015 | White |
| English Wine Project | Renishaw Hall Classic Cuvée 2017 | Silver | 2017 | White |
| Exton Park Vineyard | RB28 Blanc de Noirs NV | Silver | NV | White |
| Giffords Hall Vineyard | Giffords Hall Classic Cuvée 2018 | Silver | 2018 | White |
| Grange Estate Wines LLP | The Grange PINK NV | Silver | NV | Rosé |
| Gusbourne | Brut Reserve 2016 | Silver | 2016 | White |
| Gusbourne | Rosé 2016 | Silver | 2016 | Rosé |
| Harrow & Hope | Blanc de Blancs 2015 | Silver | 2015 | White |
| Harrow & Hope | Brut Reserve No.5 NV | Silver | NV | White |
| Hattingley Valley Wines Ltd | Blanc de Blancs 2014 | Silver | 2014 | White |
| Hattingley Valley Wines Ltd | Classic Reserve NV | Silver | NV | White |
| Hendred Vineyard LLP | Hendred Brut 2016 | Silver | 2016 | White |
| Henners Vineyard | Henners Brut NV | Silver | NV | White |
| Henners Vineyard | Henners Brut Rosé NV | Silver | NV | Rosé |
| Hidden Spring Vineyard | Classic Cuvée 2018 | Silver | 2018 | White |

| | | | | |
|---|---|---|---|---|
| High Clandon Estate Vineyard | High Clandon Euphoria Cuvée 2016 vintage Brut | Silver | 2016 | White |
| Langham Wine Estate | Blanc de Blancs 2017 | Silver | 2017 | White |
| Langham Wine Estate | Corallian Classic Cuvée NV | Silver | NV | White |
| Langham Wine Estate | Pinot Meunier 2018 | Silver | 2018 | White |
| Marlings Vineyard | Marlings Sparkling Rosé Brut | Silver | NV | Rosé |
| Mereworth Wines | 2018 White From White | Silver | 2018 | White |
| Nutbourne Vineyards | Nutty Vintage Brut 2017 | Silver | 2017 | White |
| Pamela Morley | Priors Dean Flint Hill Sunset 2017 | Silver | 2017 | White |
| Polgoon Vineyard | Seyval Blanc Sparkling 2017 | Silver | 2017 | White |
| Raimes English Sparkling | Blanc de Blancs 2016 | Silver | 2016 | White |
| Ridgeview | Blanc de Noirs 2015 | Silver | 2015 | White |
| Ridgeview | Rosé de Noirs 2016 | Silver | 2016 | Rosé |
| Roebuck Estates | Rosé de Noirs 2016 | Silver | 2016 | Rosé |
| Sixteen Ridges Vineyard | Signature Cuvée 2015 | Silver | 2015 | White |
| Southcott Vineyard | Southcott Brut NV | Silver | NV | White |
| Sutton Ridge Vineyard | Sparkling Rosé 2018 | Silver | 2018 | Rosé |
| The Squerryes Partnership | Squerryes Blanc de Blancs 2016 | Silver | 2016 | White |
| The Squerryes Partnership | Squerryes Brut 2017 | Silver | 2017 | White |
| The Uncommon | Bubbly White Wine 2020 | Silver | 2020 | White |
| Three Choirs | Three Choirs Estate Reserve Blanc de Noirs 2014 | Silver | 2014 | White |
| Vranken-Pommery Monopole | Louis Pommery England NV | Silver | NV | White |
| Welcombe Hills Vineyard | Ophelia - Rosé English Sparkling Wine 2019 | Silver | 2019 | Rosé |
| Westwell Wine Estates | Naturally Petulant 2020 | Silver | 2020 | White |
| White Castle Vineyard | Esmae Rosé 2017 | Silver | 2017 | Rosé |
| Wiston Estate Winery | Rosé 2014 | Silver | 2014 | Rosé |
| Wiston Estate Winery | Wiston Brut NV | Silver | NV | White |
| Woodchester Valley | Reserve Cuvée 2017 | Silver | 2017 | White |

| | | | | |
|---|---|---|---|---|
| Albury Organic Vineyard | Albury Estate Blanc de Blancs NV | Bronze | NV | White |
| Ashling Park Estate | Ashling Park Blanc de Blancs NV | Bronze | NV | White |
| Ashling Park Estate | Ashling Park Rosé NV | Bronze | NV | Rosé |
| Bearley Vineyard | English Sparkling 2018 | Bronze | 2018 | White |
| Bee Tree Vineyard | Bee Tree Blanc de Noirs 2017 | Bronze | 2017 | White |
| Biddenden Vineyards | Ortega Demi-Sec 2018 | Bronze | 2018 | White |
| Biddenden Vineyards | Pink Sparkling 2017 | Bronze | 2017 | Rosé |
| Bluebell Vineyard Estates | Hindleap Classic Cuvée 2015 | Bronze | 2015 | White |

| | | | | |
|---|---|---|---|---|
| Bow in the Cloud Vineyard | Cloud Nine Sparkling 2016 | Bronze | 2016 | White |
| Busi Jacobsohn Wine Estate | Busi Jacobsohn Cuvée Brut 2018 | Bronze | 2018 | White |
| Calancombe Estate | Blanc de Noirs 2017 | Bronze | 2017 | White |
| Camel Valley Vineyard | Camel Valley 'Cornwall' Brut 2018 | Bronze | 2018 | White |
| Carr Taylor Wines | Rosé 2015 | Bronze | 2015 | Rosé |
| Chapel Down | Rosé Brut NV | Bronze | NV | Rosé |
| Chapel Down | Three Graces 2016 | Bronze | 2016 | White |
| Chet Valley Vineyard | Skylark 2019 | Bronze | 2019 | White |
| D'Urberville Vineyard | D'Urberville Classic Cuvée 2016 | Bronze | 2016 | White |
| D'Urberville Vineyard | D'Urberville English Sparkling Rosé 2018 | Bronze | 2018 | Rosé |
| Davenport Vineyards | Pet Nat 2020 | Bronze | 2020 | White |
| Denbies Wine Estate | Denbies Blanc de Blancs 2014 | Bronze | 2014 | White |
| Dunesforde | Solaris 2018 | Bronze | 2018 | White |
| English Wine Project | Renishaw Hall Classic Cuvée Rosé 2017 | Bronze | 2017 | Rosé |
| Exton Park Vineyard | RB23 Rosé NV | Bronze | NV | White |
| Fenny Castle Vineyard | Fenny Castle Blanc de Noir 2017 | Bronze | 2017 | White |
| Mereworth Wines | 2019 Sparkling Rosé | Bronze | 2019 | Rosé |
| Ridgeview | Bloomsbury NV | Bronze | NV | White |
| Ridgeview | Cavendish NV | Bronze | NV | White |
| Sandridge Barton Wines | Sparkling Blanc 2017 | Bronze | 2017 | White |
| Sixteen Ridges Vineyard | Pinot Noir Sparkling Rosé 2015 | Bronze | 2015 | Rosé |
| The Uncommon | Bubbly Rosé Wine 2020 | Bronze | 2020 | Rosé |
| Three Choirs | Three Choirs Classic Cuvée NV | Bronze | NV | White |
| Tinwood Estate | Rosé 2018 | Bronze | 2018 | Rosé |
| Trevibban Mill | Black Ewe White Sparkling 2018 | Bronze | 2018 | White |
| Trevibban Mill | Blanc de Blancs 2014 | Bronze | 2014 | White |
| Vagabond Wines | Pet-Not 2019 | Bronze | 2019 | Rosé |
| Westwell Wine Estates | Westwell Blanc de Blancs 2013 | Bronze | 2013 | White |
| Wolstonbury | Wolstonbury Chalk Charmat 2020 | Bronze | 2020 | White |
| Woodchester Valley | Cotswold Classic NV | Bronze | NV | White |
| Woodchester Valley | Rosé Brut 2018 | Bronze | 2018 | Rosé |
| Woodreed Vineyard | Hunter 2018 | Bronze | 2018 | White |
| Woolton Vineyard | Chardonnay Pet-Nat 2020 | Bronze | 2020 | White |

**For further information on Award Winning English Sparkling Wines, visit:**
www.iwsc.net
www.winegb.co.uk
www.internationalwinechallenge.com
www.decanter.com

# INDEX

## CLEAN COCKTAILS

Spencer Matthews
ISBN: 9781910821411

## GARDEN WILDLIFE ON TRIAL

Ruth Binney
ISBN: 9781910821299

## AMAZING & EXTRAORDINARY FACTS: GREAT BRITAIN

Stephen Halliday
ISBN: 9781910821206

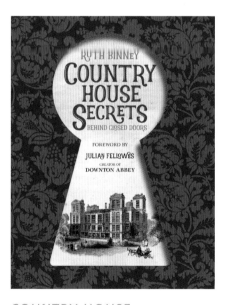

## COUNTRY HOUSE SECRETS

Ruth Binney
ISBN: 9781910821312

Discover other fascinating titles on our website at www.rydonpublishing.co.uk